RECEIVED

JUL 2 4 2022

PRAISE FOR *LIMITLESS*

"Sharing her journey with authenticity and vulnerability, Mallory doesn't just bring us into her heart—she empowers us to reflect on our own journey, finding the power that exists when we honor our truth. At its core, *Limitless* is a reminder to all of us of the strength of the human spirit to overcome circumstance."

FRANK MARSHALL, FIVE-TIME ACADEMY AWARD-NOMINATED FILMMAKER
AND MEMBER OF THE US OLYMPIC & PARALYMPIC HALL OF FAME

"Mallory is a hero and an inspiration in every sense of the word. Her story is written with such truth and authenticity, it will have you crying, laughing, and learning all at the same time. In these pages, she shares the true power of showing all those around you, including yourself, grace and forgiveness. Mallory's story, heart, passion, and faith will leave you feeling like you, too, can change the world."

MISSY FRANKLIN JOHNSON, FIVE-TIME OLYMPIC GOLD
MEDALIST AND AUTHOR OF *RELENTLESS SPIRIT*

"*Limitless* teaches us about the grit and tenacity it takes to keep coming back and harnessing the inner power to realize our own limitless potential."

BILLIE JEAN KING, FOUNDER, BILLIE JEAN KING LEADERSHIP INITIATIVE

"It's said, the measure of a person is not whether they fall but how they get back up and continue forward. In *Limitless*, Mallory shares her story of how she refused to allow circumstance to define her, but rather utilized it to redefine limitations and pave her own path forward. I have been fortunate to hear Mallory speak to many groups within Delta, and I am thrilled many more people will come to know her inspirational story. Now, more than ever, we need Mallory's message of hope and determination in overcoming adversity. *Limitless* will not only inspire you but empower you to find your own inherent strength within."

ED BASTIAN, CEO, DELTA AIR LINES

"Mallory has embodied the true sense of overcoming any obstacle that presents itself. Whether physical or mental, *Limitless* teaches us all that choosing hope over fear will conquer anything. Such a great reminder for anyone at any age . . . it is our responses not our circumstances that ultimately define us in the end. This universal message is a must-read for the world today."

CHRISTINE FARRELL, CEO, WASHINGTON SPEAKERS BUREAU

"*Limitless* is a beautiful and powerful journey of the human spirit that teaches us good will always overcome and our limits in life should only come from within ourselves."

KYLE CARPENTER, USMC MEDAL OF HONOR RECIPIENT AND
NATIONAL BESTSELLING AUTHOR OF *YOU ARE WORTH IT*

LIMITLESS

LIMITLESS

THE
POWER OF
HOPE
AND
RESILIENCE
TO OVERCOME
CIRCUMSTANCE

MALLORY WEGGEMANN

WITH TIFFANY YECKE BROOKS

NELSON
BOOKS

An Imprint of Thomas Nelson

Published in Nashville, Tennessee, by Nelson Books, an imprint of Thomas Nelson. Nelson Books and Thomas Nelson are registered trademarks of HarperCollins Christian Publishing, Inc.

Thomas Nelson titles may be purchased in bulk for educational, business, fundraising, or sales promotional use. For information, please e-mail SpecialMarkets@ ThomasNelson.com.

Scripture quotations taken from The Holy Bible, New International Version®, NIV®. Copyright © 1973, 1978, 1984, 2011 by Biblica, Inc.® Used by permission of Zondervan. All rights reserved worldwide. www.Zondervan.com. The "NIV" and "New International Version" are trademarks registered in the United States Patent and Trademark Office by Biblica, Inc.®

Any internet addresses, phone numbers, or company or product information printed in this book are offered as a resource and are not intended in any way to be or to imply an endorsement by Thomas Nelson, nor does Thomas Nelson vouch for the existence, content, or services of these sites, phone numbers, companies, or products beyond the life of this book.

ISBN: 978-1-4002-2347-3 (ePub)
ISBN: 978-1-4002-2348-0 (audiobook)

Library of Congress Control Number: 2020950321

ISBN: 978-1-4002-2346-6 (HC)

Printed in the United States of America

21 22 23 24 25   LSC   10 9 8 7 6 5 4 3 2 1

For my parents—who have guided me, giving me the faith to know that good overcomes and the courage to believe that I can make a difference. Your strength to let go twice as parents is what led me forward and allowed me to pave my own path.

To my husband, Jay—your love is more than I could have ever dreamed imaginable. You are my anchor and the light that guides me home, showing me that love perseveres all.

And to you, reader—wherever you find yourself in your own journey, may you know that you are worthy of all things splendid.

CONTENTS

INTRODUCTION

Good Overcomes

As I positioned myself on the starting block, mentally prepping for my first race of the 2019 World Para Swimming Championships, I was suddenly hit with the realization that it had been nine years since I competed at a world championships, seven years since I won a major international medal, and three years since I last raced internationally. I'd become a thirteen-time world champion and Paralympic medalist less than four years after my paralysis at age eighteen and later endured a second injury that nearly cost me my career. As I waited for the horn to sound, I felt the weight of a journey that included the darkest season of my life, but I also felt myself emerging—out of all those years of grief, struggle, and doubt—into the light I saw ahead. *You've got this*, I thought, settling into my starting position. *Whatever happens, you've got this.* The horn blared, and I pushed myself off the starting block with all my might.

A mere 34.76 seconds later, my fingers touched the wall and my head rose above the water's surface. The London Aquatics

Centre was filled with cheers and splashes as the final swimmers pushed through their last strokes. Lifting my goggles, I glanced to the scoreboard where it flashed for a moment before the final rankings appeared on the screen. There it was: *M. Weggemann, 1.* First place.

Immediately, I looked to the stands to find my team standing in their predictable order: my coach pacing on the observation deck above, my family seated below with my dad on one end, my husband on the other, and my mom in between them. We locked eyes, and my mom flashed the same thumbs-up she has given me both before and after every race of my career. I knew that thumbs-up meant "I love you," but it also meant something else, an unofficial Weggemann family motto that had gotten us through even the most trying times: *good overcomes.* I grinned and waved, and they stopped hugging everyone within reach just long enough to wave back.

Those little rituals comfort me. They are things I can count on even if everything else goes haywire. I know my family is there, as they always are—as they always have been. They were there for my first meets back after I was paralyzed; they were there for the world records and the 2012 London Paralympics; they were there for the awful years after my arm injury, when I contemplated retirement. And they were there that night, as I claimed my fourteenth world championship title. A Team USA rep wrapped the American flag around me, and I proudly raised it above my head. Despite the cheering that reverberated in the swimming complex, I could only hear two words as the gold medal was slipped around my neck a few minutes later: *good overcomes.*

My mom has leaned on the wisdom of "good overcomes" for as long as I can remember. In the weeks following my paralysis, it became her automatic response when we were faced with yet another challenge that seemed insurmountable. Mom still reminds me that with every setback, every obstacle, and every frustration we encounter, individually or as a family, "good overcomes" means that we *will* find a way forward. She is careful not to use it as a sunshiny, pat response to gloss over difficult issues, but it is her way of reminding us that as long as we hold on to our faith and surround ourselves with the love and support of others, even the darkest of days will clear and we will find light on the other side.

Life rarely offers us answers to its tests. Sometimes, the biggest challenge is simply to figure out how to make meaning of the obstacles each of us will face. When I first came home from the hospital after becoming paralyzed at the age of eighteen, I looked around my old bedroom at the artifacts of a life that felt so distant from the one I was now living. My mother sat next to me on the bed, wrapped her arms around me, and whispered, "Good overcomes." I'm not sure I believed her yet, but I didn't have much else to cling to in that moment.

Over the ensuing months, I read everything I could get my hands on about life as a paraplegic—how to adapt, what to expect, and what my future might feasibly look like. One article that stood out to me in particular cited the frighteningly low statistics about spinal cord injury patients obtaining a college education, finding a fulfilling career, getting married, and establishing a family. I don't remember the specific numbers, but what stuck with me was the deep, terrifying realization that all the things I took for granted as a natural part of my future had just been wiped away—at least statistically speaking—in an instant.

As I struggled to accept the reality of my situation, my parents did their best to comfort me. They couldn't offer an answer to my repeated questions of why, but my mother reminded me of that one piece of wisdom to which she clung: good overcomes. It was a small comfort in the moment, but I gradually recognized the wisdom behind Mom's words. Quick fixes and neat resolutions aren't always realistic. Challenges may knock us flat again and again, odds may be stacked dizzyingly high against us, and the world can seem so wildly unfair that we are tempted to give up. But life is about the long game, and what seems overwhelming in the moment could very well be pointing us toward something greater. It's up to us to push past the noise of our present, past the expectations placed upon us, and into the boundless possibilities of our unwritten futures.

My family saw a small glimpse of my mom's words proving true when I raced in my first swim meet following my injury. For the first time since my paralysis, we began to move forward together with hope as our guide.

When I first started swimming post-paralysis, I wasn't looking for medals or setting my sights on breaking world records. I just wanted to see what I could do—how far I could take my mind and my body. And when I realized I could swim without functioning legs, I thought, *who was to say I couldn't do a thousand other things too?* Swimming opened up a new life for me—it allowed me to imagine the possibilities rather than focusing on the limitations. I don't like to say that swimming allowed me to move on, because I can never move on from my paralysis; it will always be a part of me. I prefer to say that swimming helped me find a way forward—to build a new reality limited only by my own decisions, resolutions, and mindset.

We have no way of knowing where the future will take us; but, as my mother reminded me, we just have to trust that there is something beautiful waiting for us if we can find the courage to move toward it. It's like the quote often attributed to Martin Luther King Jr.: "Faith is taking the first step even when you don't see the whole staircase."

I never dreamed I would find more meaning and freedom in life *because* of my struggles, but as I enter my third Paralympic Games, I'm now surer of myself, as both an athlete and a woman, than ever before. I have shed the restrictions placed on me—by others as well as myself—and built a life rooted in possibility, potential, and promise. When I refused to accept limits to what I could do, I threw open the door to a life that's bigger and fuller than I could ever have imagined.

This, I believe, is what my mother meant when she told me, "Good overcomes." It's not about naive optimism; it's about believing in the power of resilience—the combination of courage, passion, patience, and perseverance—to create something meaningful out of difficult circumstances. Resilience is simply doing what you have to do for as long as it takes. You don't have to do it with grace, and you don't have to do it with cheerfulness—you just have to *do it*. It's simultaneously that simple and that profoundly difficult. It's also the only way to move beyond whatever limits life may have placed on you.

When we remove every boundary that hems us in—physical, emotional, or societal—we become limitless. When we reject preconceived notions about what something "should" look like, we move ourselves toward the possible. The real secret to overcoming setbacks is developing the wisdom to know which goals are worth pursuing and which weights—expectations, limitations, and disappointments—we must let go in order to rise to the top. Don't be afraid to cut anchor. Fight your way back to the surface. And, most importantly, don't lose hope that good, as it always does, *will* overcome.

ONE

YOU CAN CHANGE THE WORLD . . .
BUT YOU CAN'T DO IT ALONE

"You see this, girls?" Dad asked his three young daughters as he gestured out his window toward the sweeping stretch of wheat that extended to the horizon in every direction.

We saw it, and we knew what was coming. "This is the bread-basket of America," Christin, Jessica, and I chanted along with him, cracking up. Whether we were in the prairies of North Dakota or making our way through the southern parts of Canada, wherever Dad saw vast fields, he made the same comment, for three weeks straight—every summer. We were a sight. Our family of five loaded up in the Suburban with two car-top carriers as we made our way west from our home in Minnesota. Dad was wearing his canvas bucket hat that made its appearance each summer for our family road trips; Mom was sitting in the front seat with the map sprawled out on the dashboard, shaking her head. Each year the trip varied a little, but it always brought us to the Canadian Rockies—one of our favorite places in the world.

As children of the nineties, my older sisters and I didn't have technology to keep ourselves occupied, just one another and whatever game we could make up in the moment. The script was the same every year: Jessica and I sat in the middle; our biggest decision was whose legs took the inside and whose took the outside as we sprawled across the middle seat playing Barbies and making up our own secret language. Christin, the oldest, always had the back seat all to herself. She is seven years older than I am, and Jessica splits us in the middle; therefore, in Christin's eyes, she had already paid her big-sister dues and got the luxury of a whole row for herself and Nancy Drew.

Those trips defined my childhood in a lot of ways. My dad wanted nothing more than to share his love for the outdoors with us girls, and my mom wanted to carry on one of her favorite traditions of family road trips, so they spent all year anticipating and planning for our summer camping adventures. My mom is the queen of preparation, so she would spend weeks making packing lists, planning activities for the car to keep us occupied, double-checking that she packed our tapes (remember when that was how we played music?) and the ultra-high-tech converter for playing CDs through the tape deck, triple-checking our first aid kit, and, of course, packing the trusty green bin that housed all our snacks for the days on the road.

All these years later, I have come to realize the important lessons my parents instilled in us amid the jokes and family bonding as we navigated west each summer. Since we camped the entire way, we weren't bound by the tyranny of hotel reservations; instead, when we came to significant junctions or forks in the road, my parents would turn to us and ask, "Girls, which way: left or right?" We decided together, as a family, which path we wanted to take. At the time, it just seemed like part of the adventure, but now I can see it was actually a valuable lesson in adaptability. From the second row of the family Suburban, I learned that life isn't always about following a predetermined path, but making choices in the moment and rolling with whatever comes when the course changes.

When we were children, my sisters and I moved as a unit—whether we were running around gathering sticks at our campsite to build a fire or make a fort for the slugs (Jessica's favorite), I looked up to the two of them and, in true little sister fashion, wanted to do whatever they were doing. I wanted to be exactly like my big sisters, so I carefully copied everything they did—and not just on our road trips. Christin began swimming in middle school, and soon after Jessica did too. At first, I was just known as "Little-Little Weggie" around the pool deck, toting around my bag of coloring books and sprawling out in front of the window looking over the pool deck. But it didn't take long before I decided to follow in my sisters' footsteps, which meant more practices and races for my parents. Still, they never missed a meet and were always the loudest in the stands. The swimming community became our second family, and I felt every bit at home in the pool as I did in my own house. Being a swimmer was part of my core identity, and my sisters' too. Our parents embraced it, as they did everything we pursued, wholeheartedly.

Despite our busy schedules of swim practices, piano lessons, schoolwork, and church youth group, every evening our family would sit down at the kitchen table together and have dinner. It didn't matter if we had to eat late because Mom was working a twelve-hour shift at the hospital where she was a nurse, or if we had to eat early to accommodate our extracurriculars, we always sat down and talked about our day as we shared a meal. My family is big on rituals and traditions, and dinner was no exception. Every month as Mom wrote out the family calendar, she rotated through each person's initials so that all three of us got our own special days where we sat in the designated "special spot" and got to select the evening prayer. When I was preparing for my first communion and learning the Lord's Prayer, I took my special days as an opportunity to practice and stumbled through until I got it perfect. Dinner probably got cold some nights as my family waited until I was satisfied with how the prayer came out, but in true Mallory fashion, I was determined not only to get it right but to do it by myself.

From the time I first learned to talk, my favorite phrase was "I do it." I had two doting parents and two older sisters always ready to step in and help, so my independent streak bristled at the constant babying. At two, I refused assistance on everything from getting dressed to building block towers to fearlessly leaping off the side of the pool into the water. By the time I started kindergarten, "I do it" had become a family joke; it was my unofficial motto for life.

My family's rituals were a comfort to me and to my sisters, because we could count on them even if everything else went haywire. Like my mother's motto "good overcomes," my father had a saying he repeated to us every night as he and Mom tucked us in: "You are the best, you can make a difference, and you can change the world."

As a child, I never fully understood the weight those words carried; I just accepted them as true. Each night when my parents tucked me into bed, I was reminded that I wasn't just loved, but appreciated and supported—lessons that proved vital as I grew older.

———

While my early childhood was filled with memories of cruising through the foothills of the Canadian Rockies, my later adolescence was shaped by something far less blissful.

In middle school, I was less consumed with popularity contests and gossip, and more occupied by an awareness that my strong, smart, and beautiful oldest sister, Christin, was struggling through an eating disorder. It took her years of residential treatment, hard work, and perseverance, but by the time Christin was in her early twenties and I was in high school, it seemed she had started to turn a corner. And then the bottom dropped out of our lives.

Throughout the fall of 2005, while Jessica was away at college and I was coming into my own as an upperclassman, Christin was hospitalized due to major complications following a surgery. Despite all her progress, she had recently been diagnosed with an underlying stomach condition: gastroparesis—one of those big medical words that really just means your stomach isn't digesting food properly. She needed a feeding tube to help her stomach work, but the surgery took a sudden and drastic turn for the worse.

"Mallory Weggemann—are you still in here?" called one of my high school guidance counselors as she stuck her head into the locker room. It was just before noon on Halloween of my junior year of high school; I had just finished gym class and was changing to go to lunch. My heart sank. I knew immediately from her voice that something was wrong with Christin, and I walked out of the locker room to see my father in the hall, in tears.

The twenty-minute drive to the hospital felt like an eternity. Neither of us were able to speak. Finally, just before we stepped onto the elevator at the hospital, he turned to me and took a deep breath. "I want to prepare you for what you're about to see," he said quietly. "Christin is in the ICU, and she is hooked up to a bunch of different machines and monitors. Mal." Dad's voice caught as he tried to speak the next words gently, "She's fighting for her life."

As we walked into the room, the terror in my father's eyes suddenly made sense. There was my oldest sister, lying motionless on the bed, with her feeble heartbeat on the monitor. Mom was holding Christin's hand and crying. Jessica joined us a few minutes later, having left her college campus as soon as she got word, and our pastor arrived soon afterward. Together we stood around Christin's bed as our pastor led us in the Lord's Prayer while the nurses prepared to wheel her out for another surgery. Suddenly, faintly, Christin's voice joined in: "Give us this day . . ." My heart filled with hope; maybe, just maybe, that was her way of saying she was still there and still fighting. I thought back to those nights at the dinner table when Christin chimed in to help me as I struggled to remember the words to the prayer we were reciting together now, and I smiled. She didn't open her eyes or say anything else besides the whisper of the prayer, but that moment gave us all something to hold on to as we watched her roll down the hallway to the operating room.

It wasn't the same as a fork in the road in southern Canada, but at that moment, when we all felt the weight of unimaginable loss looming over us, we made a choice as a family to embrace each moment as we fought together to help Christin find her way back to herself again. She survived surgery that day, though many difficult years and several more brushes with death marked her recovery. It felt so unfair, watching her battle with courage and strength through her eating disorder, only to be met with profound health complications due to a completely unrelated condition. I watched as my brilliant sister struggled to regain her memory; I prayed for my "Sistin" (as I called her when I was young) to remember who I was. My heart ached as I watched her fight to learn how to talk again, build the strength to walk on her own, and piece her life together—but she did pull through and emerged healthy, whole, and unbelievably strong on the other side.

My family's faith in one another never wavered, and neither did my father's words to us each night: "You are the best, you can make a difference, and you can change the world." He wanted his girls to believe those words deep in their souls, so he never stopped reminding us of those truths, even if his voice shook a little as he said it. Seeing both the strength and the vulnerability of my parents through the ups and downs of Christin's battle comforted me because I knew I would never be alone, no matter what happened in my own life.

———

There isn't really such a thing as going back to "normal" after trauma, because somewhere along the way your perception of normal changes based on your experiences. This was certainly the case for my family. By my senior year of high school, while Christin was still battling to restore her health, I came down with a severe case of mono that never fully resolved; eventually, I was diagnosed with chronic fatigue syndrome, followed by a case of shingles. These health struggles were incredibly frustrating, but not as devastating as they might have been had I not already witnessed Christin's courageous battle. My senior year was hardly the experience I'd always hoped for. While I had the honor of serving as one of the captains for our high school swim team, my deteriorating health (not to mention the emotional stress of my personal life) took its toll on my body. Still, there was something comforting about the water—a place where I found solace and that welcomed me as I navigated through the unbearable realities our family was facing. The water was my escape, somewhere I simply put my head down and focused on the black line that trailed the pool floor below me. It was a space where I could just *be* without worrying about everything and everyone else around me. Little did I know then how instrumental the love I built with swimming would become in my future.

I think that's one of the biggest lessons I learned as a teen: we will all face circumstances that aren't ideal, when we are dealt a hand that is more than what we feel we signed up for. But we always have a choice: Do we focus on the pain, or do we choose to see the love that surrounds us? We can decide not just how we move forward, but the way we perceive the world. We can choose to see heartbreak, loss, and hopelessness, or we can choose to see the beauty and believe that we are the best, we can make a difference, and we can change the world.

Despite my dreams of going to college out of state, I put my plans on hold and enrolled at a local community college to take my general education credits. I could transfer later, I reasoned. I relied on the emotional support of my parents as I began a series of epidural injections to help treat the horrific nerve pain I experienced. While my shingles rash resolved, my nerves reacted as if they were still infected, causing a condition called postherpetic neuralgia, which resulted in searing pain. I was prescribed a series of three treatments spaced out over six months, with the last one scheduled for Martin Luther King Jr. Day—January 21, 2008. The first two went as expected, and I was up and about the following day, feeling like my old self again. So I had no reason to think that the final injection would be any different.

It was a gray, cloudy, Minnesota winter day as my dad drove me to the clinic for my last treatment. Usually my mom went with me, but she was on the schedule that day as a pediatric nurse, so Dad had the honors. As we walked into the clinic, I told him that Mom always came with me into the procedure room, since I've always been squeamish with needles. "I just want to squeeze your hand while they do the injection, okay?" I asked. He, of course, agreed.

A few minutes later the nurse called my name, and Dad and I both followed her back. We briefly talked through the procedure process as I got settled on the gurney, lying on my stomach with my dad standing at my head. As I waited for the injection to begin, I looked down at my dad's feet and I heard the echoing of the doctor and nurse talking, but everything after that point remains a blur. Some moments are burned indelibly in my brain in the most painfully exquisite detail, and others escape me completely or only flash through my memory in brief waves, as if my brain wants to save me from trauma but my heart can't let go.

The sterile smell of the room. The bright lights. The voices of the doctor and nurse. That jarring sound of my legs suddenly dropping lifelessly to the table and the jolt of pain. Then . . . nothing.

My heart began to race. Something was different—maybe not wrong, but definitely different. I looked to my dad as he held my hand reassuringly. Moments later, the staff wheeled my gurney into the recovery room, where I was supposed to sit and wait for the numbing medication to wear off. But as the hours ticked by and the feeling didn't return to my legs, we realized that something wasn't right.

"That's perfectly normal," the medical team assured us whenever we asked a question. "Just give it a few more hours."

The afternoon wore on. Finally, my dad turned to me and said calmly, "Sweetie, I'll be right back." And he stepped out into the hallway.

"Annie," I heard my dad say in hushed tones as he spoke with my mom over the phone. "Something isn't right. I'm worried."

My heart sank as I overheard him describing my symptoms. This couldn't be happening. Not again. My family had far too many memories in the hospital over the past few years. Determined not to give in to my fears, I shook away the bad thoughts and smiled as Dad came back into the room. "It is just taking a little longer than normal, but it's fine," I told him, praying my words would prove to be true.

When 4:45 p.m. rolled around and my condition hadn't changed, a representative from the clinic informed us their building was closing and I would need to be transferred to the hospital across the street for further observation. Dad had been calling Mom with periodic updates all afternoon, but with this piece of news, she knew in her gut that something serious had happened. "I'll be right there," she told him.

Moments later, the nurses came to transfer me, wheeling my bed through the tunnel under the street that connected the clinic and the hospital. When we reached my new room, I looked into the bright sterile lights above me as one of the nurses gently grabbed my shoulder and rolled me to my side, then onto the backboard she had slid beneath me. I felt the cold plastic on my shoulder blades and upper back, but beyond that I felt nothing. "3, 2, 1," the medical team counted out as they lifted me onto my new bed. Moments later I heard my mom's voice as she greeted my dad in the hallway. I couldn't hear what they were saying, but they were talking in the all-too-familiar tone I recognized from when Christin was at her worst.

That first night I felt numb, not just in the literal sense since I didn't have feeling from my waist down, but emotionally. Every voice that flooded the room sounded as if it echoed in the distance. My heart felt empty as I looked at my body, as if my soul was crying but my mind was too dazed for the tears to surface. For the next few hours, I lay there willing my legs to move, to feel something, to wake up, to do *something*.

Over the following days, we sought answers but only found more questions. All I knew was I walked into a clinic a few days prior and I never walked out. Instead, I was admitted to the hospital. I looked to my family, who were surrounding me with their love, and felt an overwhelming sense of heartbreak wash over me.

I lay trapped in my own body, unable to feel or move anything in my lower half; I couldn't sit up on my own, get out of bed, or even use the restroom. My parents were my biggest advocates, pushing for answers, demanding to know what happened in the procedure room—and each time coming up empty-handed. No one could tell us what happened; in fact, the hospital staff seemed determined to convince us that nothing had gone wrong at all. We later learned that I sustained a T10 complete spinal cord injury, leaving me paralyzed from the waist down with no motor or sensory function. But at the time, no one would say whether my situation was temporary or permanent—or even what "my situation" really was.

As I grappled with my new reality, I let my mind escape by remembering things that filled my heart with joy, thinking back to our father-daughter backpacking trips on the Superior Hiking Trail in northern Minnesota. My dad used to plan weekend camping trips with each of his girls; Mom would drop us off at the trailhead and pick us up a few days later. The deal was that Dad would carry all the gear, from the food to the tent, so we could simply enjoy the outdoors. He wanted us to have the opportunity to enjoy nature as much as he did, with absolutely no excuse for not climbing trees, jumping on rocks, and chasing squirrels. I recalled clearly how he always kept his end of the deal, even if it meant throwing me on his shoulders and carrying me through the woods because my legs got tired. He would hoist me up on top of the pack so I could hug his neck while we marched forward.

"Is this too heavy, Daddy?" I asked.

"I've got you, sweetheart. Don't you worry," he assured me.

Here I was, all these years later, pulling strength from that memory and those words: "I've got you, sweetheart. Don't you worry." I wasn't in this alone. Despite feeling as if the medical system had written me off, I had a family who valued me more than anything in the world. I knew we had stuck together while Christin beat every obstacle in her way, so I was sure we could weather this storm together too. As devastated and terrified as I was, I also realized that I had a choice in all of this. I could not will my legs to move, but I could wake up each morning and fight, knowing that I had parents and sisters who were rooting for me, praying for me, and fighting for me.

A week after my injury, I mentally began to turn a corner, taking back control where I could. At first it was putting on a pair of pants, an excruciating forty-five minutes of pulling a pair of extra-large sweatpants over my extra-small body. Mission accomplished. Next, I worked to transfer myself on my own, from my wheelchair to the physical therapy table. I knew that my "I do it" thinking was my best chance at making it through all this with any sense of myself still intact. A one-hour physical therapy session consisted of nothing more than me attempting to move myself from my chair to the therapy bench. "Don't touch me unless I start to fall," I insisted to my therapist, and he kindly allowed me the space to begin my fight to take back control of my own body. Of course, I didn't bring that same fierce tenacity every day; I still had plenty of moments when I felt overcome by the enormity of what I was facing. There wasn't any version of "it can always be worse" to soften the blow.

Through it all, I leaned on my family. They all brought different strengths: my parents were my rocks, constant and unshakable through all the uncertainty; Christin massaged my legs every day in an effort to help them remember the sensation of touch; Jessica always managed to give me a good laugh exactly when I needed it most. That's my family in a nutshell: We laugh a lot and we cry a lot. And we usually end up laughing while crying too. We had survived so much, and this would be no exception.

After two weeks on a medical care floor, I was transferred to a different hospital with inpatient rehab services, and the brief time outside of the walls of the hospital was refreshing. When I got settled into my new room at the rehab hospital, I discovered the simple joy of physically wheeling into the bathroom and looking in a mirror for the first time since my injury. That was my first lesson on the importance of accessibility. My previous hospital room wasn't set up to accommodate a wheelchair, which meant the only way to brush my teeth was in bed with a bucket. To go to the restroom, I had to use a bedpan since my wheelchair couldn't fit through the bathroom door. Wheeling up to the sink and looking in a mirror that tilted downward so I could see my whole body was not a luxury I even imagined. My new room on the rehab floor allowed me the power to reclaim those simple activities and the basic dignity of caring for myself independently.

Over the previous few weeks, loved ones, members of my church community, and former teammates and their families sent cards carrying well-wishes. My family helped me hang them on my wall, and my mom added pages from my senior year scrapbook next to them—pages filled with memories from family vacations, high school swim meets, and mission trips with my church youth group—as a way to fill my room with hope. Quickly, the white hospital walls came to life with color, and with each passing day the color only grew as more cards, flowers, and photographs arrived. Changing the world, as my father still challenged me every night, isn't always about shaking things up or transforming the big picture on your own; sometimes, it's about knowing when to lean on those around you to help carry you through the depths of loss. It's leaning on their strength as they help transform *your* world.

When I started my physical therapy regimen, I spent several hours each day with therapists who moved, stretched, and manipulated my legs in an effort to keep the muscles from going into atrophy. We tried every possible exercise to trigger a reconnection between my brain and my lower body. I threw myself into each session with every ounce of strength and determination I could muster. Part of it was sheer dumb optimism, of course; I refused to believe that my body wasn't going to heal completely. That simply wasn't a reality I was willing to accept yet. Besides, there was no way I was going to let my life go from "I do it!" to "You do it for me." My whole identity had been built on my proud independence.

The thing was, for what seemed like the first time ever, my "I do it" stubbornness wasn't enough to overcome the obstacle. No matter how hard I worked, my legs would not cooperate. No force of will could get them to budge even an inch. The occasional involuntary spasm gave me hope that maybe my spinal cord might be working to repair itself, so I kept pushing and praying for the day when I would be able to control even the tiniest movement below my waist again. But day after day, I ended my PT sessions exhausted, frustrated, and exactly as paralyzed as I had been that morning.

Throughout this trying time, my father's nightly encouragement to me never changed: "You are the best, you can make a difference, and you can change the world." On my worst nights, the words taunted me. *You can't even change your body. How can you change the world?* I thought. But even then I found comfort in those words. As the weeks stretched on, I began to understand Dad's challenge better than ever: I believed my pain had uniquely positioned me to do something greater than I would have ever dreamed had my path simply looked "normal." I accepted the idea that I had to have my world changed before I could hope to change the world in return. I just didn't know what that eventual world-transformation would look like. I chose to trust that there was a greater reason for my pain.

After six weeks in the hospital, I was finally released to come home. As I wheeled through the doors of my family's house, I was struck by how naive I had been when I walked out of those same doors nearly two months earlier. I yearned for that moment, wishing a piece of me had been aware enough to slow down and enjoy the effortless freedom that comes in placing one foot in front of the other, the strength that comes as you ground yourself in a standing position, the energy you feel when you place your weight on the balls of your feet. How many little things had I never noticed before they suddenly became precious, priceless experiences?

While I was in the hospital, my parents had been working on transforming our formal living room downstairs into a bedroom for me; but since it wasn't yet finished, I had to spend my first night in my old room upstairs. My mom had carried my bags up, made my bed, and prepped my cocktail of nighttime medications, which included shots I gave myself to prevent blood clots due to poor circulation. The realities I faced extended far beyond not being able to feel or move my legs. I hadn't just lost my ability to walk, but also to regulate body temperature, control my bowel and bladder function, and digest food properly. Every day it seemed as if I was learning something new that had changed with my body. But in that moment, all I could focus on was how I was going to get up the stairs.

My dad sensed my concern and pulled me up onto his shoulders. As I wrapped my arms around his neck, my mind flashed back to childhood.

Is this too heavy, Daddy?

I've got you, sweetheart. Don't you worry.

Hoisting me up onto his back, he lifted me exactly the way he had on our hikes when I was tiny and exhausted. I felt awful that my paralysis had added to the load he was already shouldering, but then it hit me: he didn't see me as a burden. I was the best, I mattered, and I could change the world—he told me so every night.

That first night home, as I stared around my room, I realized it was still in the same condition I left it on the morning of January 21. I lay in bed that night looking at my high school swim posters still on the walls, my books for the start of spring semester piled on my desk—all remnants of a life that had ceased to exist. I knew, come morning, I had a choice: I could stay holed up in my room and grieve all that I had been through, or I could lean on the strength of my family and get into my wheelchair, wheel out my bedroom door, and start fighting to piece my life back together. It was actually a very simple choice, but it was one of the biggest decisions I ever made.

The next day, I woke to the sight of my wheelchair, my daily reminder that my life was different now. But I didn't stop to muse over what it represented. I transferred into it, got dressed on my own, and wheeled out the door of my room and down the hallway. Those simple acts set the pace for the days to follow. I would choose to live. Each day, I would choose, over and over for years to come, to be more than my circumstance. And what gave me the courage to make that same decision every day was the knowledge that I wasn't in this alone. The African proverb "It takes a village . . ." rang true in every aspect of my life. I needed a village now, more than ever.

I needed the people who once partnered with my mom chaperoning youth group mission trips but now spent days working alongside my dad to build a ramp in our garage so I could get into our house. I needed the parents from our swim community who helped my dad pull up the carpet in our downstairs sitting room and install hardwood so my chair could roll more easily as they converted that space into a bedroom for me. I needed my family's friends who brought meals so my parents had one less thing to worry about as we settled into our new routines. I needed the broader community of my parents' employers and colleagues who were generous with family leave so Mom and Dad could do what they needed to support me and my sisters. I needed our dear friends from church who drove me to and from physical therapy each day when my parents returned to work. I needed my best friend, Katie, who made life feel as normal as possible each time we talked, even though deep down I knew she was grieving for me too. I needed my family, who gave me the space to feel what I needed to feel, despite the fact that January 21 didn't transform just my life but theirs as well. Before I could think about changing the world, I had to change my thinking from "I do it" to "*We* do it." Together. The shift wasn't easy to make, but it was my only way forward.

That idea served as my compass as I found myself navigating uncharted territory, uncertain what my future might hold. We all must make a similar pivot from "I" to "we" if we want any hope of recovering from setbacks, disappointments, and trauma. I had to be willing to look beyond my personal pride in tackling every obstacle that came my way and understand that some challenges are just too big to take on alone. Accepting help does not make you a burden; it makes you part of a village, a web, a network, a *family* of people whose lives are interconnected, come good or bad. There are going to be moments and circumstances that disrupt your life in ways you could have never imagined, but you can't shut yourself off from the rest of the world. Self-reliance is a beautiful trait, but only in moderation. Your journey is your own, but that doesn't mean there aren't other people who want to make the way easier for you.

Humans were meant to live in societies; community is the backbone of civilization. As I learned from watching Christin's struggles and going through my own challenges post-paralysis, the key to survival is to surround yourself with individuals who believe you *can* make a difference and change the world.

As Dad and Mom kissed me goodnight that first evening home

from the hospital, and Dad repeated his familiar phrase, I knew he spoke the truth—that my parents would always have me, that my family would always love me, and that I still possessed tremendous potential for impact. I also knew I couldn't do any of it alone—and that I wouldn't have to.

Sometimes we go through the unimaginable, but it's those very experiences that give us the drive, the reason, and the passion to go out and make a true difference in the world. Without that shake-up, we may never gain the perspective or wisdom to live into our full capacity. There's an old expression: "God never wastes a pain." I can see now, years down the road, how true that was for me. My trauma was the soil from which something beautiful would grow; I simply had to trust, wait, and keep responding to life with hope. At the time, of course, I was so consumed by the struggle that it was hard to imagine anything good coming from my pain, but that's because my vision for myself was still hemmed in by past constraints and ideas. When old parameters are stripped away, we often find that our future is infinitely greater than anything we might have dreamed otherwise, and our potential is utterly limitless.

T W O

FACE YOUR FEARS

"Here we go," my physical therapist said as she wheeled me backward down the ramp into the pool.

"I don't want to do this. I don't want to do this," I repeated, watching as my knuckles turned white while my hands gripped the arms of the wheelchair.

"It's okay, Mal," my parents assured me from the pool deck. "You love swimming. You've got this!"

We got as deep as my shins, and my fear only increased; I could see the water rise on my legs, but I couldn't feel a thing; it was as if I were completely disconnected from my own body. The only sensation I was aware of was the lump in the back of my throat as my chest began to tighten, and then the tears came pouring down my face. I'd eagerly agreed to try water therapy when I saw it on the schedule, hopeful that it would bring me comfort as the water always had.

My family, of course, was amazing. My dad even put on

swimming trunks and got into the water with me, but after only a handful of sessions I requested that pool therapy be removed from my PT rotation. All my life, the pool had been a place I felt at home. But now I felt disconnected and utterly terrified in the place that used to be my sanctuary. Everything in my life suddenly seemed yanked from my control, and I desperately needed *one* place that still felt familiar. I didn't want my paralysis to take my love of the water from me too. Yet it seemed it was happening just the same.

More and more, I was feeling out of place in familiar spaces. From a permanently seated position, everything looked different from when I stood at my full height of five foot nine. In my wheelchair I couldn't even look individuals in the eye without tilting my head up. My entire worldview, quite literally, had shifted.

Weeks earlier, when I'd been an inpatient in the hospital, I received a pass to leave for the afternoon. I had been working on learning how to put on shoes again—just one of the many daily living activities I had to relearn—so I thought the pass was the perfect opportunity to persuade my dad to take me shopping. After all, I needed to find a new pair of shoes for physical therapy, didn't I? And not just any shoes—shoes from Nordstrom at the Mall of America. But once we arrived, my brilliant plan evaporated. After spending so many weeks in the bland stillness of the hospital, I felt intimidated by the lights, noise, color, and countless people I encountered. As I looked around the mall, I saw a vast array of individuals, but not one in whom I saw myself. I didn't see anyone in a wheelchair in the window displays. No mannequins were seated in a chair like mine. None of the employees rolled up to greet us. There simply weren't any other individuals there who utilized four wheels instead of two legs. I felt alone. But even more than that, I felt invisible. My new circumstances felt foreign in my own life, and now I realized they seemed foreign within our society as well.

I could tell that other people noticed it too. They stared as I rolled by, probably playing the "What's wrong with her?" game in their heads. It was then that I realized the luxury of blending in. As talkative and social as I've always been, I've also always nursed an overwhelming fear of being in front of a crowd; I froze every time it was my turn to read aloud in elementary school, and I barely passed my public speaking class in high school. The idea of having all eyes on me usually made me shut down. But now, I would forever stand out in whatever room I was in, whether I wanted to or not. In one moment, I went from having countless other identities—tall, blonde, daughter, sister, teenager, swimmer, student—to just one. All the different ways in which people could think of me were instantly superseded by a different label: "disabled." People couldn't help but notice my paralysis first. Now, before I was anything else, I was "the Girl in the Wheelchair."

Ironically, at the same time that I desperately wanted to blend in again, I was stunned and frustrated that I couldn't see myself reflected anywhere. My wheels made me simultaneously stand out to the world and become invisible to it. I'd always heard that gender and racial representation matter, but never before had I realized that this is true for people with disabilities too. Suddenly I understood why: you can't become what you don't see. Nowhere did I see modeled a thriving, active, independent life in a wheelchair. I felt both totally isolated and completely overexposed.

Thankfully, my family helped me address some of those fears through our trademark sense of humor. On March 23, Easter Sunday, I had been home from the hospital for about three weeks. We were sitting together in the living room of our family's house, and I was showing off the new skills I had recently mastered in PT: transferring myself from my wheelchair to the sofa and back again, and pulling myself up from the floor into my chair.

"This is a big deal," I explained as I transferred myself back down again to the ground, "because it means that if I fall, I'm not helpless. I can get myself back into my chair to either get on with my day or call for help if I need to." Mom, Dad, and Christin applauded, acting every bit as impressed as I wanted them to be. Jessica, however, got a glint of humor in her eyes.

Hopping up, she suddenly grabbed my wheelchair and ran it into the foyer of the house, then came back into the living room with a bit of a smirk and said, "Sure, but your chair may not always be right next to you when you fall. Let's see you try it now!"

There was half a second of silence, and then we all started cracking up. "Fine," I said. "I'll race you!" and I started scooting myself out of the room. It was such a relief in that moment to see that my family was still teasing me exactly how they used to while acknowledging this as a huge part of my life instead of pretending not to notice it. That one little prank by my sister encouraged me to think about my paralysis as something that was okay to joke about within our family. I didn't have to be afraid of how it made me "different," or that we always had to get sad and somber when it came up in conversation, or that it made me off-limits to any joking or family teasing. At that point, I was only okay with my close family laughing with me, and no one else; but if I could blend in with my parents and sisters again, maybe I could eventually find a way to just be a normal teenager in the world around me. Maybe.

———

Three days after Easter, Mom, Dad, and I flew out to California to visit my dad's aunt, who lived in San Diego. The trip was not nearly as difficult as you might imagine, mostly because *everything* was new and complicated at that stage, so traveling was just one more facet of life we were figuring out as we went. Not only could I no longer walk, but I was still getting used to a body that couldn't fully regulate temperature and bladder function that wasn't as predictable. Awkwardly boarding an airplane was the least of my worries. The point of the trip was just to give us a little change of scenery, as well as some warmth and sunshine. But even more than the enjoyment of it, the vacation was a distraction from my nineteenth birthday on March 26.

Birthdays are usually a joyful time—a chance either to celebrate the year you just finished or to look ahead at the potential and promise of the coming twelve months. But my nineteenth birthday marked none of that. I wasn't exactly celebrating the recent changes in my life, nor was I excited about the world of possibilities that awaited me. I didn't have much hope about what lay ahead as I started this next stage of life with paralysis, so spending time rolling down the boardwalk, watching the waves, and simply enjoying the sights and sounds of San Diego was exactly the distraction I needed to help me focus on the present rather than spiral downward.

Staying in the present was one of my biggest goals at that point. In some ways, it was easy because most of what I did was aimed simply at making it through the day. I needed to teach my body how to carry me from morning to evening without giving out, and I had to train my mind to keep powering through the new obstacles and frustrations without giving up. My focus needed to be on relearning daily life, while also finding a way to not just get through my days but truly live again.

Unfortunately, it was easy for me to fall into the trap of wishing myself back to January 20, the day before my paralysis. If I wasn't careful, I ended up getting stuck in memories of all the things I couldn't do anymore—and might never do again. In those moments, the sense of loss was overwhelming. In that direction, my future stretched out before me like a bleak, narrow hallway with nothing but closed doors and what felt like impossibilities. When I tried to research what life could look like for people living with spinal cord injuries, I read statistic after statistic about how unlikely it was that I would ever go to college, have a career, get married, or live any kind of fulfilling life. Everything seemed to indicate that the odds were decidedly against me achieving any of the goals and dreams I had set for myself; it was almost as if society was encouraging me simply to give up. In one split second, something happened that took my ability to walk, and it would be years before I understood the full implications; my greatest fear was that it would also take my ability to live. As society seemed to consider me "damaged goods" or someone to be pitied, I wanted nothing more than to prove I was every bit as worthy of pursuing my dreams as any other person, no matter my physical condition.

I started journaling just a few days after my paralysis, filling notebook after notebook. If I ignored all of my worries and confusion, they just grew louder, so I put them on paper, not only to process the whirlwind of emotions raging in my head but also to get them *out* of my head and think of something else—and move on with whatever I needed to do to get through the next twenty-four hours. I couldn't change the past and I couldn't yet envision my future, so I spelled out all the grief and fear I carried each day— and then closed my journal and tried to focus on where I was in the moment.

That short trip to California over my birthday was the perfect diversion from everyday life, but I also knew it couldn't last forever. I had to return to my real life—whatever that looked like now— and find a way to begin piecing it back together as I figured out my new normal.

One Saturday morning, just days after we got home from our trip, I wheeled into the kitchen from the downstairs bedroom my parents had now completed for me. Christin sat at the kitchen table with my parents, eating breakfast, the Minneapolis *Star Tribune* spread out in front of her. "I just read an article you might find interesting," she remarked, holding the newspaper out to me. The Paralympic swimming trials for Beijing were being held at the University of Minnesota aquatics center that weekend, and it was open to the public.

"Cool." I shrugged. "What are the Paralympics?"

Writing this now, years after the fact, it's hard to admit I went nineteen years with no awareness of a movement that would become a cornerstone of my life. We looked up the Paralympics online that morning and were blown away by what we found. It was then that we learned that the Paralympic movement runs parallel to the Olympic movement but is for individuals with physical disabilities. The Paralympic Games themselves are hosted in the same city and same venues as the Olympics, with only a few weeks between Olympic closing ceremonies and Paralympic opening ceremonies. As we all crowded around the computer, we got fired up over something we hadn't known existed five minutes ago.

"This is amazing," Christin insisted. "We've got to go tonight, Mal."

Late-season flurries were in the forecast, and I had several movies lined up—or maybe it was a *Gossip Girl* season one marathon—and much-anticipated plans involving popcorn, pajamas, and vegging out on the sofa with the dog. "Nah," I told her. "I'm good."

For the past ten and a half weeks, ever since my paralysis, my family had been extremely accommodating to whatever I felt up for, so I was a little surprised when everyone immediately pushed back.

"But Christin's never helped me transfer into the car before," I insisted, determined not to leave the house. To be honest, it wasn't just the comfort of home and a warm dog making me hesitate. I had so many memories of walking—*walking*—around the aquatics center that I didn't want to replace just yet. It was one thing to read about something cool; it was entirely something else to take a deep breath and force myself to actually experience it in person—and whatever emotions it might trigger.

"I'll figure it out," my sister said. "We're going."

A few hours later, we managed to get my chair in and out of

my mom's Honda CRV without any mishaps, parked in one of the accessible spots on the University of Minnesota campus (it was still weird to realize those spots were now available to me), and made our way into the aquatics center. As we entered through the first set of doors, the scent of chlorine immediately hit me. As we passed through the lobby where large glass windows over-looked the university's competition pool, a dozen years' worth of memories hit me all at once:

Cheering in the stands for my big sisters at weekend meets.
Finally joining the team with them when I turned seven.
Watching my mom work for hours to make banners, fans, and
*   fleece boas in our team colors to hand out to the other parents.*
Writing my events on my arm in magic marker so that even
*   when I got distracted talking to everyone on the pool deck,*
*   I could remember when I was supposed to race.*
Passing bags of Sour Patch Kids down the bleachers with
*   teammates as we waited for our events.*
Hearing my parents in the stands with cowbells.
Seeing my parents in their predicable spot, side by side, with
*   Mom flashing her traditional thumbs-up.*
Feeling the safety and comfort of the water, where all my
*   problems could be forgotten for a little while.*

As stubborn and independent as I was, swimming had never been about competition for me; it had always been about joy in the most basic sense. I had been good but never great; I swam varsity all four years in high school and was even named captain as a senior, but I never qualified for state championships. That wasn't why I swam. I relished the community, friendships, and freedom the pool offered. No matter what was going on in my life—typical adolescent worries or legitimate fears about my sister's health—I could bury myself over the black line and just swim. I could trust the black line; all I had to do was follow it, and I knew it would lead me directly to the wall. There was no question, no uncertainty, no twists or pitfalls or unpleasant surprises. The pool was my sanctuary, and the sights, the sounds, and the excitement were an indelible part of my childhood and the life I used to have.

In that moment, as we entered the pool area, the sensation that overwhelmed me most was the scent. Chlorine smells exactly the same no matter where you are in the world. In the midst of everything else that had just been upended in my life, the fact that something could still remain completely unchanged was staggering. I paused and allowed the memories to wash over me. Surprisingly, I wasn't filled with regret or a sense of loss. It was as if the muscle memory of my brain reawakened, thanks to the familiarity of my surroundings. This wasn't a dull, depressing therapy pool I'd encountered in the hospital, but a loud, colorful competition pool churning with athletes. And not just any athletes. These were athletes who looked like *me*.

As each heat of swimmers took to the blocks, wheelchairs, crutches, and prosthetic limbs were all discarded. In the water, it was just a swimmer and their body, exactly the way it always was. These individuals weren't sad or hindered by their "disability," and they certainly weren't people who were to be looked at with pity for the difficult hand life had dealt them. These were strong, dynamic, and elite athletes who absolutely relished their lives and their incredible abilities.

"Christin," I breathed, when I finally managed to move again. "Let's go closer."

We wheeled into the stands and along the top deck. I leaned as far as I could over the railing to watch each race, scarcely believing what I was seeing. My heart filled with awe and excitement and an overwhelming sense of hope.

"Do you think I could do that?" I asked her as the horn sounded and eight swimmers dove into the water in a flash.

"Why not?" She shrugged.

I smiled—one of my first genuine smiles in nearly three months—and replied with words that proved tremendously prophetic. "Maybe in four years I could be here, competing at Paralympic trials."

That was the first time I gave myself permission to consider something in my future—the first time I asked myself "what if," looking ahead, rather than allowing those same two words to pull me back to that traumatic day in January.

Moments later, a woman approached us and asked if we were enjoying the meet. "I can take you to the pool deck and introduce you to some of the athletes and coaches afterward, if you'd like," she said, noticing how I could barely tear my eyes away from the athletes. That was how I first met Barb Popovich, mother of Paralympic legend and eventual US Olympic & Paralympic hall-of-famer Erin Popovich.

Barb explained some of the finer points of Paralympic swimming technicalities and answered the dozens of questions fighting to be the first one out of my mouth. After the meet, true to her word, she escorted us down to the deck where we met, among others, Jim Andersen, the club coach at the University of Minnesota. He'd had a swimmer competing in trials that night, and he was happy to talk to me about what opportunities might be available to me too. "If you're interested, come by Monday afternoon for practice," he said. I couldn't stop beaming.

I returned home that night a completely different person from the one I had been when I left. After almost three months of feeling broken, rudderless, and isolated, I suddenly saw capacity, direction, and community—and I wanted it more than I had ever wanted anything in my life.

Less than forty-eight hours later, my dad and I arrived back at the aquatics center and made our way down to the deck where Jim—Jimbo, as everyone called him—was getting the team ready for practice. I introduced my dad and we chatted just a minute, then Jimbo turned to me and said, "Well, go put on your suit and let's get you in the water."

My heart stopped. *Put on my suit? Get in the water? I thought we were just talking today.* I hadn't even brought a suit. I wasn't ready to get back in the water; I just wanted to learn more about what might be out there for me. I could feel myself starting to retreat back into that place of fear and uncertainty, but just then I heard, "Hey, Mal! What are you doing here?" as my former high school teammate and then Minnesota Gopher swimmer Roxanne came striding over to me on her way out of the locker room. As soon as she heard my predicament, she immediately laughed it off. "No problem," she said. "I've got a spare suit, cap, and goggles that you can use. Let me grab them."

Before I knew it, she had me set up with everything I needed. But I couldn't bring myself to put them on; I just sat and stared at that suit laid out on the bench in front of me. It was one thing to talk about wanting to do something, to feel excitement about a possibility, to fall in love with an idea; it was entirely something else to actually do it. Right now, I knew I was facing an enormous moment of decision. Was I going to allow myself to stay comfortably in the realm of the hypothetical or face my fears, take the risk, and make this dream real? What if I panicked again, the way I had in the therapy pool two months ago? What if the water was no longer my safe place? What if all the excitement I felt about this crazy swimming idea proved pointless, and the hope that had been bubbling up inside me for the past two days evaporated and made me feel even emptier and more broken than before? *What if I never had the courage to find out?*

That was the moment I learned the value of follow-through, no matter how frightening the prospect.

It doesn't matter how great our ideas are if we never put them into action. Our ambitions will never amount to anything if we don't take the first step toward making them a reality, even if we have to push past our fear to do so. Of course, failure is always a possibility, but we each have to decide whether we are going to live in a place of fear or a place of freedom.

During physical therapy, swimming showed me exactly how vulnerable my body had become, but now I realized that the only thing that had the power to truly paralyze me was my fear of the unknown. Would I lean into the unknown and find out what my body could do, or would I allow fear to make decisions for me?

I took a deep breath and, with shaking hands, pulled on the suit and wheeled back out to the pool deck. Transferring myself out of my chair, I sat for a minute with my legs dangling in the water. That was when my dad piped up with the Weggemann family signature move, a completely inappropriate joke during a very serious moment: "So . . . if she sinks, one of you is going in to get her, right?"

I started giggling. If my dad was joking, that meant he was nervous and uncomfortable. And if he was nervous and uncomfortable, too, it meant I wasn't alone. That was all I needed. I pulled my goggles down over my eyes, then dropped into the water.

"Just start swimming," Jimbo stated matter-of-factly, and I did. I put my face in the water and began to place one hand in front of the other as I formed a freestyle stroke. Five strokes in, something clicked, and I was immediately home once again. The pool felt the same. The strokes were familiar. Every time I pulled my body forward, I was farther away from my wheelchair. For the first time since my paralysis, I didn't need a medical device. I didn't need assistance. I didn't need anything but my body exactly the way it was. It was just me, the water, and my own power moving myself forward. By the time I reached the other end of the pool, my entire perception of myself and my view of the world had shifted. If I could do something as seemingly impossible as swimming by myself, what else might be possible?

I swam for half an hour that day. Two weeks later, I was putting in a full two-hour workout with the rest of the team. Four weeks after that, I swam in my first meet, "Jump into June," where I found myself competing against eight-, nine-, and ten-year-olds. It didn't matter to me that I finished dead last in every single race that day. I came up out of the water grinning ear to ear. I wasn't there to win; I was there to live, and that's exactly what I was doing.

There was a bit of a learning curve for all of us. I had to figure out how to adapt my strokes, how to get used to starting a race from the water rather than diving in from the blocks, and how to go into my second pool-length without doing a flip-turn to push off the wall. Jimbo had to retrain himself not to yell "Kick!" instinctively when he saw my arms doing all the work. But we got there together, and each practice and meet built my confidence more. Before I knew it, I wasn't simply relearning how to swim; I was beginning to dream. No longer was I swimming just to process the emotions of my paralysis; now, I found myself working toward a seemingly crazy ambition—to make the US National team.

I decided that spring that my paralysis was not going to be my paralyzing factor. It was not going to be the moment that stopped me from chasing goals, and it certainly wasn't going to be the moment that stopped me from living. It did not have the power to keep me locked in fear and doubt. My biggest obstacle was not that the lower half of my body no longer worked the way it once had; my biggest obstacle was being willing to face with courage the uncertainty that lay before me. There was no scenario in which my situation could solve itself—no way anything was going to change if I didn't force myself to be the catalyst for that change. I had to find a way to be okay with who I was, where I was. That didn't mean I had completely accepted my paralysis or what had happened to me; it just meant that I recognized the need to move myself into the unknown and take each day on faith that choosing to live was the right decision.

Of all human emotions, I think fear may be the most universal. Not everyone can understand what it is like to be physically paralyzed, but everyone can understand fear. Everyone knows what it is like to feel scared, to feel doubt, to feel uncertainty and insecurity. We know what it is like to be afraid to act because we fear failure, rejection, or humiliation. We can't ever hope to push past our fears if we don't first admit they are real. If we never challenge ourselves to move beyond what is comfortable and safe, we will never know what might be possible.

We all have to make these same choices, on some level, every day: Do we allow our fears to paralyze us, or do we find the courage to lean in and stare them down? Only when we face our fears head-on, do we find out what is possible beyond our limitations.

Over the summer of 2008, I decided it was time I used my swimming as a catalyst to challenge myself in the other aspects of my life, so I enrolled for classes at the community college down the street from my parents' home. When I was first paralyzed, I vowed that I wouldn't return to the classroom until I could physically step foot in one. Although swimming challenged that notion, it forced me to realize that it was okay to meet myself where I was and begin to rebuild my life. *Why not?* (That became my unofficial mantra.) If I could move my body in a pool, why couldn't I move it around a campus? If I could face my fear of the water, why couldn't I face my fear of fully integrating back into society?

Swimming became the bridge that connected me to my past as I figured out how to live my daily life free from fear or self-imposed limitations. I realized that thinking about the past didn't have to send me down a rabbit hole of grief. Of course I was sad about what I had lost, but I didn't have to define my life by it. I could live in the present and celebrate where I was right now, without feeling like happiness had to be deferred until maybe someday we figured out how to get my legs working again.

That is the challenge we all face, no matter what our obstacles or disabilities. Whether they are physical, emotional, mental, financial, social, or a trauma from our past—the type of disability doesn't matter—they are all rooted in the same thing: belief that we are limited or hampered in our capacity to thrive. And as long as we let fear drive our actions, those limitations are true. By allowing fear to call the shots in our lives, we validate every doubt, every insecurity, and everything that might hem us in or hold us back. But the moment we allow ourselves to feel hope—the moment we commit to following through instead of just talking about it, the moment we face our fears head-on and refuse to grant them any more power—is the moment we can change everything about our lives.

THREE

MOVE FORWARD

Change. What exactly is change? Our lives are all about change. Everything is about change. Change isn't easy. It can bring both good and bad. It takes a lot of work to change for the better and for some reason most of us are afraid of it. Change brings many mixed emotions . . . excitement, fear, doubt, and hesitations. I have seen my life as I knew it for *eighteen* years change in the blink of an eye, but every day I work toward turning that change into a positive.

The past month I have had to force myself to really accept that I am a paraplegic. I have been in a wheelchair for nine months now, but I have had a hard time accepting this as my new life. One moment really can change your life forever. Last year this time I never in a million years thought this would be my life now, but the reality is this is who I am.

—FROM PERSONAL JOURNAL, OCTOBER 21, 2008

Following a tragedy, we often find ourselves trudging through the depths of grief while also yearning for some sliver of normalcy. It had been nine months since my paralysis; and with that, I realized I was no longer counting in days or weeks but in months, that would soon change to years, as I approached my one-year anniversary. I struggled to accept what happened at the beginning of the year, but I knew that in order to truly move on I had to find a way to accept my new reality.

The love and support of my community were overwhelming, but so were the thin-lipped smiles. The half shrugs as people asked, "How are you doing?" The confusion in their eyes as they struggled to know how to engage with me now that my face was half a body length lower as I sat in my wheelchair. With each interaction, I felt myself confronted with the reality that my life had changed forever—and there was no escaping it.

Even in my own family, which was never anything but completely supportive and loving, the collective mourning over my past was starting to consume me. I knew what happened that day didn't just happen to me, but it happened to them as well: my dad, who will forever have the memory of watching his youngest child become paralyzed while he was helpless to intervene; my mom, who was on the receiving end of a phone call no parent ever wants to receive; and my two sisters—Christin, who had been through so much already, and Jessica, who after watching her older sister stare down death now had to watch her little sister adjust to life with paralysis. We were all grieving a loss, all learning how to accept a new reality while working through trauma, all battling to find a way forward.

As the fall went on and I successfully maneuvered my chair to and from the spot where Christin dropped me off for class, I couldn't help but reflect on the contrasts. On one hand, how incredible was it that I was already back in school taking classes? On the other hand, how vastly different was this from the college experience I had always imagined for myself?

Before my paralysis, I had set my heart on going out of state to a large university to major in journalism. After my paralysis, however, my dream of moving away was abandoned because— well, of course it was. It didn't even cross my mind for the first six months as I focused simply on getting through the next twenty-four hours, or even just the next physical therapy session. But just as my confidence returned during the fall of 2008, the memory of that plan suddenly came back, and what I initially wrote off as totally impossible now didn't quite seem so far-fetched after all.

I began researching schools with two requirements: first, somewhere warm (well, at least warmer than Minnesota); and second, a coach who was open to working with an athlete with a disability. I had heard from another para-swimmer about a program I was particularly interested in: Gardner-Webb University, a small school in western North Carolina with an NCAA Division I swimming program. I proceeded cautiously so as not to freak out my parents, just in case the whole thing fell apart. Not only was I proposing that I move almost twelve hundred miles away, but I was considering private school. Between the modifications to the house and all the out-of-pocket medical expenses my parents were facing, financial stress—which almost always follows medical challenges—was a real concern. Of course, they would never tell me, but all I had to do was listen to their late-night conversations to know that not only were they adjusting to their baby girl being paralyzed, but also to the costs that came with it. While the idea of going away to school was beyond exciting and in so many ways felt like the next step forward, I was now potentially adding a not-inconsequential tuition check to their stack of bills. Still, it couldn't hurt to look, right? Without breathing a word to my parents or my sisters, I sent in my application and reached out to Coach Mike Simpson, the head of the Gardner-Webb swimming program. Not only did Coach Simpson respond to me right away with enthusiasm about welcoming me on the team, but I heard back from the school in a matter of weeks that I had been accepted—with a significant academic scholarship.

In early November, I wheeled into the kitchen as my parents were preparing dinner and shared the news that not only was I looking at schools out of state, but that I had applied and been accepted to one. To their credit, they both had only a moment of panic in their eyes before they burst into huge smiles, telling me how proud they were and that we could absolutely fly out to see the campus in the spring. That's when I dropped the second part of the plan on them: I had applied for the spring semester, which began in early January, just over a month and a half away. I hadn't even been paralyzed for a year yet, and I was still relying heavily on their assistance to get through daily life. Yet there I was, telling my mom and dad that in a matter of weeks I wanted to move halfway across the country and start a new chapter. It was then that I realized, not only were my parents grieving alongside me, but they were learning how to let go for the second time.

Since my early teens, I had watched as Mom and Dad rose to the occasion, putting their fear aside and doing what was needed to support us girls, no matter the circumstances—and this situation was no exception. Regardless of how much fear they were filled with, they found a way to smile and come together to do what they felt was best to help me learn how to move forward. Two weeks later, Mom, Dad, and I were all on a plane headed to North Carolina. I think they understood the real reasoning behind the move as much as I did. This wasn't about trying to revive my dream of going to college away from home as much as it was about a chance for us all to move forward—them, by having a chance to fall back into slightly more "normal" roles other than caretakers; and me, by having a chance to start over in a place where I would be surrounded by new people getting to know me for the first time. No one would have to renegotiate exactly what hanging out with "Wheelchair Mal" looked like as opposed to "Walking Mal," because my new friends would only know me in my wheelchair. No one would be grieving the loss of the life I used to have, because they never knew me before my paralysis. This was my best chance to learn how to move on, on my own terms and with my new reality.

As we looked around the Gardner-Webb campus as well as one other nearby school to which I had applied, I took note of a thousand tiny things I had never thought twice about before. The most wheeling I had done was within the walls of my family's home and from the car to class or to the pool for practice. Could I navigate an entire campus independently? And just how steep was the hill between student housing and the dining hall? The size of the dorm rooms—was there room for me to navigate the space on four wheels? The entrances into buildings—could I even get into the residence hall?

Most of the places I had encountered up to that point I had known before I was paralyzed, so any difficulties I experienced in getting around were really just about having to relearn how to move my new body in that space. But this was different. Obstacles were everywhere. Thankfully, the school's administration was nothing but supportive. "If Mallory chooses to come here," the admissions officer told us, "we can convert a double dorm room to a single to accommodate her chair, add an accessible stall in the communal bathroom, and create an accessible entrance into the building before she arrives." It didn't matter that the start of the semester was barely six weeks away; we both recognized a need—me for independence, and them to make their campus more accessible—and we got to work.

My parents and I were blown away with how welcoming and adaptive the university was, but even in the excitement of this huge transition, I needed to come to terms with what all those modifications really meant. They weren't temporary fixes to make things easier for me during a period of immobility; they were permanent and necessary changes to allow me to carry out the basic tasks of daily life. The chair, with all the accessibility obstacles it brought, was now part of my life—my present and my future. I would never be able to leave my paralysis behind. It was all as much a part of me now as any other physical trait inherent to my body. Was I really ready to take all of this on?

January 4, 2009, less than one year after my paralysis, I took a huge leap of faith. I moved into my dorm and, a few days later, waved goodbye to my parents as they returned home. As the door closed and I turned to look at my new room, I took in the dozens of photos that plastered the walls—90 percent of them were of me when I was still standing. I smiled looking at all the familiar faces who had given me hugs, prayed for me, sent me good-luck cards, and cheered me on at the going-away party my parents had thrown just a week earlier—the people who had filled my hospital room with cards, flowers, and balloons; the people who supported my family and gave me hope that not all was lost; the people who added color to my life in the most literal way during the darkest hours. I felt surrounded by love, but I was also keenly aware of how alone I was.

For the first time in nearly a year, I didn't have a call button to summon a nurse if I fell. I didn't have my dad to ask to carry me upstairs to the bathroom if I wanted to take a shower. I didn't have my mom to help me make breakfast if I woke up with an aching body. Sure, there were people down the hall from me, but they weren't part of my intimate support structure. It was scary, yet also incredibly freeing. At long last, I was able to figure out exactly who the new Mallory was without anyone else's ideas, memories, or preconceived notions influencing me. I could become a person who did amazing things, not a person to whom something happened. In that moment, I reclaimed my power as an active force, rather than a passive one, in my own life.

———

I quickly fell into the role of "typical college kid." I rode with teammates to practice. I wheeled myself to classes. I ate in the dining hall when I wanted. I holed up in my room if I needed to study or just enjoy the fact that I really could be alone. I felt myself become part of the student body and enjoyed the community of people who were getting to know me on my own terms. Coach Simpson and the entire Gardner-Webb swim team were amazing, too, adjusting to my arrival in the middle of the season as if I had always been a part of the team.

When January 21 hit, the first anniversary of my paralysis, I braced myself for an onslaught of emotions, but the date actually was not as triggering as I had feared it might be. I woke up and saw a letter my father had emailed me. He wrote:

> I am going to celebrate the person that you have become, the people that you have touched and the future that is before you. You are a motivator of many, showing people that no matter what challenges you are confronted with in life, you as a person have a choice in how you confront them. Mallory, you are my hero, my inspiration, the reason that I face the world with a smile on my face. You have changed the world this past year and you continue to bless all of us with your courage. Hold your head high and celebrate the gift that God has given you; the gift of life, determination and love.

That letter was my reminder that I had a choice in what that day would mean for my future. I found the beauty that surrounded me in my little dorm room in Boiling Springs, North Carolina. It's not that I didn't think about the past—how could I not? The evidence of it was everywhere. The only option I had, then, was not to try to leave it behind me, but to learn how to let it propel me forward.

Even as my emotions raced ahead, my brain sometimes struggled to keep up. About a month into the semester, I had an extremely vivid walking dream. They rarely happen to me anymore without all the proportions looking off since I am now used to the world from a sitting height, which sends me a cue that it's just a dream. But, at the time, I still had enough standing memories that my brain was completely fooled into believing that my legs worked as they used to.

When my alarm went off at 5:00 a.m. for an early morning weight-training session, I swung myself out of bed and attempted to stand without even thinking. Instantly, my whole body dropped to the floor, and I lay stunned while I struggled to wake up fully and grasp what had just happened. When the fog and confusion finally cleared, I realized no one had heard me fall and no one was coming to help. Taking a deep breath, I dragged myself up into my chair and wheeled over to the closet to get my clothes. I was bruised and shaken, but I also just proved to myself that I was capable of taking care of *me*.

That morning, I realized in the starkest possible way that no matter how my brain might try to trick my body into thinking that my paralysis was behind me, I would forever wake each morning with a wheelchair by my bedside. I will now roll, rather than step, into each new day. Regardless of how much I yearned for life prior to January 21, 2008, I had to allow myself to find the freedom that comes in the present—the lightness that comes when we choose to stop living in the past and decide to meet ourselves where we are in the present moment. I discovered that I possessed the strength to keep doing what needed to be done in whatever capacity I was able to do it. I made it to practice on time, and I gave my all that day and every single day from there on out. That fall may have shaken me, but I knew it didn't mean I was broken. I was simply still finding the strength to put the pieces back together.

My parents recognized my progress when they flew to Atlanta for our conference championship at the end of February. From the stands, waving laminated fans with our bulldog mascot plastered on them and handing out fleece boas my mom had made in Gardner-Webb's colors, Mom and Dad watched me navigating the pool deck with a whole new confidence. Even more than that, though, they watched as I interacted with my team as a full competitor and member of the squad. While I was the only athlete moving about in a wheelchair, not just on our team but at the entire meet, I began to realize that my disability was as much a part of me as the fact that I have blonde hair; it's part of what makes me uniquely me, but it doesn't define me.

I had been welcomed by a coach and embraced by the team for who I was—I just happened to race with a wheelchair sitting behind my lane, and our team bus had a lift. Simply put, I was just Mal, and my parents saw that too. They told me later that they could sense a difference. It was as if they were finally starting to see the old Mallory again—but more than that, they were seeing me bridge my past to my present, even as I looked toward my future. We were all intimately aware that what happened on January 21, 2008, had changed my life, but as we began to heal, we realized that it didn't change who I was—it only deepened me. I was still the same bubbly, outgoing, goofy Mal; I had just been overshadowed by trauma for some time. Once that cloud began to lift, we realized that not only was the old Mallory returning but a new version was emerging with it. That day didn't change who I was, it just redirected my path to allow me to grow into who I was meant to be.

One month after Atlanta, I competed at the Can Am Para Swimming Championships, where I was nationally classified, making me not only eligible to make the US National Paralympic team but also to break American records. I celebrated my twentieth birthday just days prior to the start of competition. As I ushered in a new decade of life, I marveled at all the changes of the past few months and everything the future promised—on my own terms, not anyone else's. Not only did I make the US National team at that competition, but I felt the power that comes with accomplishing the impossible. Now I wanted to see what other limits I could shatter. Next up? Representing Team USA at world championships.

Following my paralysis, I found myself on the receiving end of an outpouring of unsolicited opinions from society. People seemed to think that their curiosity trumped my right for privacy. I felt as if everywhere I turned, society wanted to tell me that my accomplishments were wonderful, but anything shy of devoting my life to walking again was me giving up. It was as if the only outcome that constituted *true healing* was me standing at five feet, nine inches tall once again and placing one foot in front of the other. This challenged my faith and, most of all, it challenged my view of my own self-worth. If I allowed myself to look backward, I was told I was living in denial and needed to accept my new reality; yet, if I allowed myself to look to my future with dreams and ambitions, I was told I was giving up too quickly.

I learned that grief comes in many shapes and sizes, and our path forward happens on *our* timeline, not anyone else's. With each success, no matter how minor, I found confidence in the decisions I was making for my own life. Not only was I hopeful for what my future had in store, but I was dreaming again—unapologetically choosing to pave my own way.

With the World Para Swimming Championships now on my radar for the fall, I was faced with a difficult decision: Should I throw myself headlong into training for them or continue my life as a student-athlete at Gardner-Webb? After quite a bit of agonizing, I finally decided that the right path for me at the time was to return home that summer, take classes at the University of Minnesota (the "U"), and focus my energy on chasing my goal of not only making the world championship team but becoming a world champion myself. As much as I loved Coach Simpson and my teammates, I had accomplished exactly what I had set out to do when I moved to North Carolina; I proved I could make it on my own without the safety net of my family nearby. Most of all, my semester in North Carolina taught me one incredibly important lesson I wasn't expecting: the difference between moving on and moving forward.

Going into my time at Gardner-Webb, I had it in my head that I needed to find a way to move on, but now I realized that was impossible. We don't simply move on following trauma—how can we? January 21, 2008, and the days and months that followed will forever be a part of me; I can't simply move on from them as if they never happened. I have four wheels beneath me to remind me otherwise. What I can do—what any of us can do following a trauma—is move forward, carrying the lessons from my trauma with me the same way I carry the wisdom gained from my positive life experiences. Over the course of my semester at Gardner-Webb, I had found the courage to not only hope for but truly *believe* in something again, which was exactly the spark I needed to help launch me toward whatever my future had in store.

At the end of the semester, I sold my futon, TV, and microwave, packed the rest of my stuff, and flew home with my dad, settling back into my same old bedroom. When I left school, I feared that returning home would feel like a step backward, but as I unpacked my clothes and settled back in, I realized that this move was one of the largest steps forward I had taken. I had only been gone for four months, but I came back feeling the freedom that comes with letting go, accepting my reality, and giving myself permission to move forward with it.

I picked up my training routine at the U with Jimbo right away, and that persistence paid off when I raced in a local club meet and broke my first American record, the 100-meter butterfly, a few weeks later. That record marked only the beginning, not the end, of my goals. I was taking charge of my life. I was setting goals and exceeding them. The transition out of survival mode was complete; my decisions in the present were being steered by my future, not my past. Instead of focusing on how to get through the day, I was beginning to dream of what might lie ahead. What steps did I need to take to get myself ready for international competition? Could I break another American record? A world record?

———

With every victory, whether in the pool or simply in learning how to live life independently, my body's limitations seemed a lot less restrictive. I now recognized the freeing truth that my life—even my very sense of self—could be defined by something more than my paralysis. It will remain a part of the fabric of my being, but it doesn't have to define who I am.

Loss is an inevitable part of life, but we must all learn how to move forward from where we are with what we have. Moving on was impossible because I couldn't simply leave my paralysis in the past any more than any of us can simply forget a trauma we have experienced. When we make moving on our goal, we set ourselves up for failure because it's not a viable goal. We can't rewind or erase the past. Moving forward is our only real option. We rebuild our lives with our new identities, incorporating the empathy we've gained, the wisdom we've earned, and the strength we've discovered. We carry those lessons with us, and we become fuller, more complex people *because* of our experiences, not in spite of them.

I had to find myself again in the midst of my circumstances. I had to recognize who I had become, and who I was still becoming, in order to step from one chapter of my life to the next. Not only did this allow me to redefine myself, but it also allowed the people around me to redefine their own roles. When I returned home to Minnesota, I no longer needed the safety net my family had provided, and they no longer felt they needed to fill that role for me. Instead of loss and uncertainty, we now had an opportunity to move forward together in love and empowerment.

For so long, my family and I operated on hope of better times to come and faith that we would eventually find our way forward, and that served us well for a season. But now, with trials for World Para Swimming Championships in Edmonton, Canada, slated for later that summer, I had more than just hope in my arsenal. I had an unshakable confidence that stemmed from a belief that good was finally overcoming—and the future was mine to decide.

FOUR

LIMITLESS

Why not me? I thought as I pushed through the final 25 meters of my 100-meter butterfly at the Can Am Championships in Edmonton, Canada. It was July 30, 2009, and I'd just experienced a spark of clarity in the final meters of my race—an awareness that in that moment I was in full control of what happened in the coming seconds. I had the power to control my destiny. Someone had to win the race, so why not me?

I dove my hands for the final stroke as the word *forward* pulsed in my brain. *Forward* wasn't just a reminder anymore of maintaining momentum throughout my race, but a reminder that looking forward was the only place to focus as I pieced my life back together.

My hands reached the wall and I grabbed the edge of the pool. As I lifted my goggles, it took a moment for my eyes to focus on the screen: 1:20.14 WR. *Wait a minute, does that say what I think it says? Are those two letters after my time—*

"Mallory Weggemann sets a new world record!" The announcer's voice echoed through the swimming complex as the arena filled with cheers.

Why not me? I thought again as I grinned from ear to ear, flashing a smile up to my parents as I returned my mom's thumbs-up with one of my own. Honestly, the significance of breaking a world record hadn't yet set in; I was focused on the fact that I had just dropped a few more seconds off my time from my last meet. I had turned it into a game with myself: if I could physically excel—if I could continue to get faster with each race—then I must not be all that "disabled." Who cared about breaking records when I could break the glass ceiling I felt had been placed on my capabilities?

Jimbo gave me a high five, then told me to cool down so my body could recover for tomorrow's races. After all, it was only day one of a three-day meet. Before we left the pool that night, the 100-meter butterfly was already in our rearview mirror, and we were squarely focused on tomorrow's events: the 50-meter freestyle, 200-meter individual medley, and 400-meter freestyle—my favorite. We had trained all summer for this competition, three months of two-a-days in the pool and dry-land strength training. I quickly learned that being physically strong wasn't enough; I also had to focus on my mental fortitude—learning how to tune out noise and distractions, including other people's very limited beliefs in what I might be capable of doing. Turns out, my "I do it" stubbornness fueled my greatest secret weapon: a determination never to back down. I set my sights on eventually competing in all seven individual events, and I was close to achieving that goal.

Back at the hotel, my dad went to pick up dinner for us while my mom and I called family to share the exciting news. As I logged on to my laptop to post on Facebook (after all, did it even happen if there isn't a social media post?), I also started to clean out my email inbox. I quickly began to mark all the spam to delete it when something caught my eye: "NBC Today Show Interview?"

Wait, seriously? No. That's got to be some spambot trying to steal my credit card info. But maybe? It wouldn't hurt to open it, right?

"Oh my goodness, no way!" I shrieked, just as my dad returned with our pizza. Quickly reading the email, I summarized for my parents. "I've been invited to appear on the *Today Show* on Sunday morning! They saw the story that our local station ran last week about me and they want us to come to New York City!"

As we sat in our hotel room in Edmonton, the magnitude of what had happened that day—not just the record, but the overall sense of "We're really going to be okay"—began to break over us. We were no longer fighting to get through each day; we were simultaneously living and thriving as we worked through the grief. I wasn't struggling with how to put on my shoes or get myself dressed anymore; I was now the fastest woman in history in the S7 100-meter butterfly.

Over our pizza that night, my mom smiled at me and said the same words she had been saying for years: "Good overcomes." It was her way of reminding me to hold on to faith when I didn't know what the road ahead might bring; and, in that moment, it had never seemed truer that good really does overcome.

"Do you think I can do it again tomorrow?" I asked my parents as we got ready for bed.

"Do what, sweetie?" my mom responded.

"Break another world record."

My parents looked at each other, then my dad shrugged. "Why not?"

Mom nodded, then added, "You have made it this far. You, my dear, can accomplish whatever you set your mind to."

And with that, I rolled over and let myself dream—not just of another world record, but of *all* the possibilities my future held.

"It doesn't look like there are any itineraries to get us to New York in time to make the early morning taping on Sunday," my dad said as we left for the pool the next morning. "It looks like our only option is to skip finals on Saturday. Is that something you're willing to do?"

I didn't have to weigh my choices very long. It was a chance to appear on national TV to talk about my journey. I imagined what it would have meant for me, lying in my hospital bed eighteen months before as I questioned my own capabilities, to see someone in a wheelchair being celebrated for breaking boundaries. Hope would have been more than a hypothetical concept—hope that my body, changed as it was, was still capable of tremendous things. I could have *seen* that reality instead of simply imagining it.

"Absolutely," I told him. "Let's do it."

When we arrived at the acquatic center, my parents took their place in the stands while Jimbo and I made our way onto the pool deck so I could begin my warm-up. Our impending trip to New York City was exciting, but I had to shift my focus to my races.

I was now posting times that were breaking records and ranking me number one in the world, but I was very much the "newbie" on the pool deck. I was still learning all the intricacies of the Paralympic swimming world, like classification. Since not every athlete has the same impairment, we are divided into classifications; for swimming, there are ten different classes for physical impairments, with S1 being for swimmers with the most significant impairment and S10 for those with the least severe. First, you get nationally classified (as I had six months prior), but in order to compete internationally you ultimately must go through international classification, which makes you eligible for not only international competitions but world records and being entered into the world rankings. It is a complicated process. The easiest way to understand it is by thinking of it like weight classes in wrestling. Our "weigh-in" is our classification appointment, where classifiers review our medical records and the physical capabilities of each athlete's body in relation to competition. That week leading into the start of competition, I underwent my international classification and was placed in the S7 class, which encompasses a number of physical variations.

At times, all this felt like another language—an influx of new information that was hard to understand while I continued to learn more about my paralysis. For me, all that really mattered was that racing felt like another opportunity to take control of my destiny and move further away from the trauma that launched me into the adaptive sports world in the first place.

Friday evening, as I dove into the water for the 400-meter freestyle finals, I stared down every inch of the black line below me, lap after lap. When my hand finally met the wall, I realized I had just chased down a nine-year-old world record that had been standing since the Sydney 2000 Paralympic Games. Forget breaking the glass ceiling—why acknowledge any ceiling at all? As far as I was concerned, the sky was the limit.

In that instant, all the voices I'd heard when I was first paralyzed drowned out. Every person—even myself—who told me my future would be full of obstacles, restrictions, and limits was silenced. I felt more powerful than I had ever felt in my life. It was as if a recording was playing over and over in my head: "I get a choice in this. I get a choice in this." For the past year and a half, people had been projecting their ideas onto me of what my life should look like and what my future would hold; however, that day in Edmonton, I knew I not only had the choice to shake them off but also the power to do so.

Each success I had was about so much more than just swimming; every record I broke in the pool was another perceived limit I silenced. I found myself repeating my own words: *the only limits you have are the ones that you create—you've got this, Mal.* My future wasn't for anyone else to decide. I was haunted by the reality that I didn't have a choice in my paralysis and that I couldn't have done anything to change that day. But maybe it was all part of a larger plan, and in order to find out what lay in store for me, I had to stop letting others limit my potential. Who cared what anyone else thought about what I could or couldn't do? This was *my* life and these were *my* dreams, and I couldn't wait to see just how far I could take myself.

Saturday morning, I swam in prelims for the 100-meter freestyle and secured my spot as the top S7 swimmer in the world for the event. I ended my time in Edmonton with four world records, six American records, and six number one world rankings. I hated to miss finals, but that meet had already given me so much. As I wheeled out the doors that afternoon with my mom and dad beside me, I felt the stillness of that moment. Here we were all these years later in the Canadian Rockies again, and we were still making decisions at each fork in the road: left or right, fight or fold. I didn't have all the answers, and I still carried loss in my heart, but each opportunity was a choice in which direction I wanted to take my life. I left Edmonton knowing I had the power to pave my own way.

Thankfully, our flight to New York had a layover in Minneapolis, so as my mom and I made our way to the next gate, my dad exited the arrivals area to meet Christin, who was waiting with a bag full of fresh clothes for us. Dad gave her a quick hug and told her to pass one on to Jessica, too, then snaked back through security and sprinted to our flight.

New York was more than I could have possibly hoped for. I had never been to the city, and now I wasn't just visiting as a tourist but as a guest on the *Today Show*. The lights, noise, busyness, and buzz of the city were absolutely electric. Coming off the high of my performance in Edmonton, everything felt unreal. When we arrived at the studio that morning, they ushered all three of us into hair and makeup. For months, I'd felt insecure and timid; I honestly could not recall the last time I felt beautiful. But as I rolled on set that morning, I felt not only beautiful but powerful as I donned my Team USA national team jacket and prepared to talk about everything my body could do. As Jenna Wolfe, the host, asked me about my dreams and goals, she posed one question I had never put much thought to until that moment: *Would I change what happened on January 21, 2008, if I could?*

Without thinking about my response, I immediately answered no, which came as a shock even to myself. But I realized in that moment that while I wasn't sure yet as to the reason for my paralysis, I believed with all my heart that there *was* a reason, and I would find a deeper purpose because of the circumstances I had faced.

After our taping, my parents and I made the most of our time in New York. I had always wanted to tour Central Park, but I quickly realized it wasn't as easy to navigate in a manual chair as I might have hoped. Instead of despairing, however, we quickly settled on a solution that proved to be even better than the original plan: a horse-drawn carriage ride. I visited Times Square and shopped at the stores I'd only ever seen on TV. And all the time, I couldn't help but marvel at the fact that even though I'd had eighteen years of walking in which I could have made a trip like this, I was doing it now in a wheelchair. In some ways, I was actually doing it *because* of the wheelchair, and I loved every minute of it. As the cherry on top of the trip to the Big Apple, I received official notification that evening that I had been named to the 2009 World Championship team, meaning that in three months I would be representing Team USA in Rio de Janeiro on the international stage. *I'm living*, I thought on the plane ride home. *I'm really living life, paralysis or not.*

While I was in the hospital immediately after my injury, I made a list of things I wanted to do when I walked again—before deciding to chase that list whether I was walking or not. Already I had checked off not only returning to the classroom but moving away for college and competing as an NCAA Division I athlete, and now that list had expanded to realities I never imagined possible. Some were as dramatic as breaking multiple world records, while others were as mundane as learning to drive again. Before leaving for Edmonton, my parents bought me a new car with adaptive hand controls installed, so the next order of business was for me to learn how to drive utilizing my hands for the break and accelerator rather than my feet. I surprised myself with how quickly I got the hang of it. One August morning, just a few weeks after I got home from New York, I passed the road test at the DMV, then I dropped my dad off at home and drove myself to the U for practice.

I drove myself. It's such a deceptively simple sentence and such a deceptively simple act, but it was huge to me. I was taking charge of my life. The transition out of survival mode seemed complete; my decisions in the present were being steered by my future, not my past. What steps did I need to take to get myself ready for the fall semester at the U? What did I need to do to make myself stronger as I set my goals for the world championship? How could I leverage both my swimming and interest in journalism into a career both in and out of the pool? I could imagine life with more clarity and less fear than even a few months ago. It seemed impossible that everything had gone off course so drastically just a year and a half prior, and now it was suddenly taking off in a new and unbelievably exciting direction.

The compressed time frame became especially apparent to me that fall when my former Eagan High School swim coach Steve Van Dyne arranged, with support from the rest of the team, to surprise me with a banner hung in honor of my accomplishments at the school pool. My parents and I arrived at the final meet of their season simply to support the team. The upperclassmen on the team were all underclassmen my senior year when I was captain, and I thought it would be fun to go back and support them and see old friends and teammates. It wasn't until Steve made an announcement asking me to come down to the pool deck at the end of the meet that I realized there was anything special going on. Wheeling onto the deck at the very pool where I'd first fallen in love with swimming, I couldn't believe it had been two years since my last meet there as a student. Two years isn't that long in the scheme of a lifetime, but those years had changed my entire world. The pride I felt that night wasn't just about the banner; it was about staying true to myself even when my circumstances gave me every reason to drift—it was a reminder of where I came from and how much that anchored me in who I was choosing to become.

That evening, I saw a number of people I hadn't seen since before my injury, which made me a little nervous. I was all too aware of how much my reflection in the mirror had changed, and I could only imagine how much more striking the difference must have been for other people to see me wheeling instead of walking for the first time. To combat that, I anchored myself in how far I had come and allowed the confidence I had tried so hard to rediscover shine through. It wasn't my responsibility to make people feel okay with my paralysis, but I did want to remind them that I was still the same person. I know some of them were surprised to see how well I was doing—laughing, thriving, and seemingly loving my life. To be honest, I was a little surprised as well. For more than a year, I'd been holding my breath, looking for any and every small victory I could claim as a sign that everything was going to be okay. I hoped that things would get better (whatever "better" looked like), but I never really let myself progress beyond feeling cautiously optimistic. But now, that hope was turning into belief. I didn't just *want* my life to have direction and significance; I now had faith that it would, and that I had the power to make it happen. And nothing drove that point home more directly than the Short-Course World Para Swimming Championships in Rio de Janeiro late that autumn.

We flew to Brazil on Thanksgiving. It was my first time traveling with Team USA, and everywhere I looked, I found another reason to be hopeful that I could build an independent life—but, even more, I found reasons to be *proud* of who I was and this community of which I was a part. Before leaving for Rio, my family armed me with a pair of red high-top Converses inside of which they had written messages of encouragement. My parents and Jimbo traveled to Rio, and my sisters cheered me on from Minnesota. Every day—between the messages in my sneakers, the cards they'd packed for me to open each morning, and the traditional thumbs-up from my mom in the stands—I knew that I wasn't on this journey alone. Everywhere I turned, I saw subtle reminders that my community was right there with me, every stroke, over the course of six days of competition. I won five golds representing Team USA, and I can't begin to describe the pride I felt sitting atop the podium, listening to our national anthem, and watching the American flag rise.

My parents brought a video camera to Rio, and one clip in particular stands out to me. My dad struggled to track me as I swam the 400-meter freestyle, but my parents' voices come through clearly as I touched the wall for my finish.

"Annie, she did it!" my dad cheered.

"She sure did, honey," my mom said, her voice choking with emotion.

In that moment, I became a world champion for the first time; and as I sat atop my first international podium, my parents watched proudly as the American flag was raised and Christ the Redeemer, Rio's most famous statue, illuminated in the sky in the distance. I will forever treasure that memory not only because of what it represented for me, but because of the joy in my parents' voices in the video. Swimming didn't just bring me back to life following my paralysis; it also gave my parents a place to heal.

A piece of my heart was mended in Rio, and not just because of my performance. After my paralysis, I felt alone, confined to the view of what others perceived I was (or wasn't) capable of doing. But at the 2009 World Championships, I felt seen. While in Rio, I had the honor of rooming with my teammate Cheryl Angelelli, a woman who despite becoming a quadriplegic as an adolescent had gone on to compete in three Paralympic Games. Cheryl was a beacon of hope for me. She showed me a path forward by allowing me to see what I could become. Like me, she had been injured as a teenager, yet there she was in her early forties, married, a homeowner, and with a full-time career outside of the pool. She had everything, did everything, and was everything I had been told wasn't possible for "people like us."

I also met Kirsten Bruhn, a German competitor who was in her late thirties and still dominating the sport. She, too, had a story similar to mine, and watching her thrive in her body exactly the way it was—not as some compensation prize for a "whole" life on two working legs, but completely comfortable in her own skin as she went out and slayed in whatever she did—I saw what I dreamed for myself down the road. It felt like I had discovered a light for my path forward. The future I wanted wasn't just hypothetical. Real people *like me* were out there living in ways that were often more full, productive, and flourishing than people without any visible disability.

When I returned home, I had a new goal: live on my own. Like, *entirely* on my own—not in a dorm. I had a small amount of medal money, and I felt empowered. After all, if I could be a five-time world champion, surely I could manage living by myself.

After some discouraging phone calls to places that weren't wheelchair accessible, I stumbled onto a furnished studio apartment being sublet while the tenant who leased it studied abroad. It was close to the University of Minnesota campus and, most importantly, close to the pool. Christin came with me one afternoon to check it out, and I fell in love with the place instantly. It was nothing fancy, but it had everything I needed; even better, it was available for the spring and summer. I signed the lease, took a few measurements, and then went home to once again drop the news on my parents that I was moving in three weeks. Thankfully, they handled it just as well as they had the previous year when I announced my desire to move to North Carolina. In fact, I think they may have been expecting it this time. I was never one to shy away from a challenge, and my "I do it" mentality was just as strong at twenty as it had been at two.

Not long before the second anniversary of my paralysis, I moved into my apartment and began the spring semester at the University of Minnesota. I was balancing my days between morning practices, classes, lifting sessions, afternoon practices, cooking meals, and juggling a social life—all the while still maintaining laser focused on my swimming. The 2010 World Championships were coming up that summer in Eindhoven, the Netherlands, and I wanted nothing more than to not only continue shattering the perceived limits that had been placed on me but prove they never truly existed in the first place.

My ambitions weren't limited to the pool, though; I was also a full-time student that spring, and I had just been accepted into the journalism program at the U. I was enjoying life as a college student again, feeling challenged by my classes and making new friends. Living on my own excited me; it gave me the confidence to realize that not only could I break down boundaries in the pool, but I could do the same outside of the pool. I was now doing everything that just a year prior seemed impossible: living on my own, driving, attending college, making new friends and socializing on campus, and excelling in the pool in ways I could have never dreamed possible. I even began dating again.

I ended the spring semester with the confidence that I had the power to create my own destiny. Sometimes we feel so confined to a predetermined path that we become weighed down by the burden of expectation, or worse, are left with no expectation at all. Although it was hard for me to accept at first, I quickly came to realize that society's complete dismissal of what I could do was a blessing rather than a curse, because it gave me the freedom to create my own future the way I saw it. Being limitless, to me, meant that instead of sinking to someone else's ideas of who I should be, I had the strength to rise to my fullest potential.

One day in July, I went to the Nike store at the Mall of America to design a pair of Team USA–inspired shoes to wear to Worlds. As I tinkered with the color options in the design studio, one of the employees came over and offered his help. Our chatting quickly turned into flirting and before I knew it, I left the store with not only a pair of shoes but also his phone number.

We talked quite a bit over the next few weeks, and then, one day, he asked if I'd like to get dinner some evening.

"Um, sure. Yes. I'd love to," I stammered, trying to sound calm.

"Great! It's a date," he said.

It's a date. Holy cow, it's a date! My mind raced. It seemed like the entire world was opening up to me, if I was just willing to take the chance.

I bought myself a new dress for the occasion and carefully straightened my hair instead of just throwing it up into the swimmer's bun I usually wore. Chad greeted me with flowers and took me to a fancy restaurant downtown. Afterward, we wanted to keep talking, so we went down the street to a bar with an outdoor patio. Summer was in full swing in Minnesota, and it was a beautiful evening. "I'll get the drinks," I told him, feeling confident— radiant—as I wheeled myself to the bar to order.

A table full of guys in their forties wearing business suits stood around a high-top, surveying the space and talking among themselves. "Who would want to date a girl in a wheelchair?" one of the guys asked his friends as I passed.

I was already too far away to hear their answers, but it didn't matter what they said. Just like that, the spell was broken. Here I was, an athlete with nine world records and more than twenty American records, and one throwaway comment made me feel absolutely worthless, as if nothing I did counted for anything. My accomplishments and accolades didn't matter; people still saw me as less-than, inferior, someone to be pitied or even mocked.

In that one instant, a hundred other memories came flooding back to me: offhand comments people had made about what a "tragedy" my life was; well-intentioned but ultimately hurtful remarks about how sad it was to see my potential wasted, as if I would never accomplish anything again in my life because I now relied on a wheelchair. As I mumbled my order to the bartender,

I recalled one particular moment from the prior year. I was waiting in line at the grocery store, playing peekaboo with the toddler waiting in front of me. We were both giggling, and she seemed pleased by the fact that she could look me almost directly in the eye from her seat in the shopping cart instead of having to look up at me like she had to with all the other adults around her.

"I can tell you love kids," the mother said, her face sad as she gestured towards my wheelchair. "I'm sorry you'll never get to have children of your own."

Shocked at her words, her presumptions, her pity, I dropped my hands from my eyes and sputtered a reply. "Well, I mean, you never know. Besides, there are lots of ways to make a family."

"Oh, I know, honey," the mother said with a sigh, in what I could only assume she believed was a kind voice. "But, really, what kind of mother could you be?"

I snapped back to the present as the bartender placed two glasses in front of me, and I balanced them carefully on my lap as I turned around to wheel back to my table. The guys in suits were focused on something else now, completely unaware and unconcerned that their casual words a minute ago had cut me to the bone. I held it together through the end of the date, but when I was alone in my apartment at last, I fell to pieces. Was I fooling myself to believe that I would ever be anything other than "the girl in the wheelchair"? Who would ever love me as I was? Who was I to think that I could build an active, dynamic future on my own terms, when the first—and maybe the only—thing anyone ever saw was my physical brokenness?

But are you broken, really? My brain pushed back. *Could a broken person do what you've done? Could a broken person have the discipline to train the way you have and the resilience to keep pushing toward new goals?*

I caught a glimpse of my arms in the mirror. They were more muscled than they had ever been in my life. *Are broken people stronger than before?* I challenged myself.

I looked at the books and the stack of lecture notes still on my desk from spring semester. My medals hung on a hook above my computer. *Do broken people continue to stretch their mind and push their creativity? Do broken people challenge themselves to keep chasing excellence?*

Then I noticed the flowers my date had brought me, now arranged in a vase on my counter. *Do broken people choose to put themselves out there, despite society telling them they are unworthy?*

There it was—not just the flowers but everything that surrounded me in the little home I had made for myself. I was more than what some woman in the grocery store assumed about me. I was more than some offhand comment in a bar. I was more than other people's assessments of my worth or my abilities or my aspirations. It wasn't outrageous to believe I deserved love and respect. It wasn't a reach to think that I could have a fulfilling life. My hopes and dreams were no less valid than anyone else's. Of course, that didn't mean I was guaranteed success—no one is—but it did mean that I owed it to myself to try. What is brokenness anyway, except someone else projecting their own insecurities onto what they imagine your worth to be?

Alone in my cozy sublet apartment on that warm night in the summer of 2010, I suddenly recognized that the way I saw myself contrasted greatly with the way the world saw me. So many people around me were still trapped by the ignorance and stigma surrounding one small part of my physical body. My instinct was simply to ignore the disconnect, until I realized that I couldn't expect people *not* to see my wheelchair. I chose, instead, to focus on changing *how* they saw my disability—that it's a core part of my identity, not something to be pitied or wished away.

I knew I had a choice to make. I could live limited by other people's perceptions of what I could or should do, or I could pursue the life I wanted. It wasn't about the medals or the records, but about believing in my own worth enough to chase my goals with everything I had in me. And that's true for all of us. When we draw our identity from our own passions and core values rather than someone else's expectations, only then are we able to fulfill our greatest potential. Of course, there will be times when we question the struggle or days when we don't feel up to the task, but it's up to each of us to turn our excuses into fuel. When you catch yourself saying, "I can't do this because . . . ," ask whether you really believe that or if you are just settling for someone else's idea of what you should be. It may seem hard today, but you know what's even harder? Living the rest of your life boxed in by other people's restraints.

Society is really good at projecting its own insecurities onto us—all of us. Anything that might be different from whatever we've collectively decided is "normal" becomes a prime target. Who hasn't been told our dreams were too big or too out of the ordinary, or our voice was too loud or too quiet, or our vision of ourselves too much or too inaccurate to matter? Who hasn't been made to feel unworthy or ashamed for wanting to live our truths?

The hardest thing about my injury wasn't the physical part, but accepting the fact that even though society saw a label permanently stamped on me, that did not mean I had to accept the preconceived notions that came with it. I did not have to live the kind of life a person with a disability was "supposed" to. I did not have to conform to anyone else's narrow, simple idea of what "disabled" should look like. The moment I realized *I* held the key to my destiny, I truly became limitless.

And Chad called me two days later and asked me to dinner again. I was chasing the life I wanted, and it turned out that some people thought *I* was worth chasing too.

FIVE

HEALING IS NOT CHRONOLOGICAL

All it took was the familiarity of the procedure room, and in that moment, I flashed back to January 21, 2008—regardless of how hard I tried to stay in the present I couldn't fight it. I have prayed for years to be able to let go of those memories, to tuck them within the pages of my journal and move forward, but here they are resurfacing, reminding me that healing isn't chronological. The truth is, it doesn't follow a neat timeline—it surfaces on a random Tuesday, with no forewarning. It has been almost three years, in that time I have become a 13-time World Champion, yet all it takes is for me to close my eyes and my mind can replay every detail of that day. No success in the world can erase what is ingrained in our hearts; instead of running from the traumas of our past we must find the space to honor them as a reminder of all we have weathered.

—FROM PERSONAL JOURNAL, NOVEMBER 5, 2010

WELCOME TO COLORADO.

I freaked out a little inside as Christin and I sped past the sign, the afternoon sunlight glinting off the metal. We'd been driving all day—our second day on the road—but we still had a little time until the sun set behind the Rockies. My parents were miles behind us in a rented minivan full of IKEA furniture I'd bought before I left the Twin Cities. My internet sleuthing had revealed to me that Colorado didn't yet have an IKEA in August 2010, and what self-respecting Minnesotan moves into a new place without a carload of modular Swedish furniture?

This move was just the latest in what had almost started to feel like a nomadic lifestyle. But the fact was, I had committed myself completely to my career, which meant that I had to go where the best training opportunities led me. And right then, they were leading me to the Olympic Training Center (OTC) in Colorado Springs.

It had only been a few weeks since I returned home from the 2010 World Championships in the Netherlands, and at this point, my parents were my biggest cheerleaders. When my sisters and I were children, they never missed a swim meet, driving all over the state to cheer us on; this was no different, only now they were travel-ing the globe to support me as I chased my dreams. While my sisters hadn't been able to join us for an international competition yet, I knew they were there in spirit. In fact, Christin had started a tradition: she would send me, with a container of homemade cookies, a card for each day I was gone.

Now, as she and I made our final approach into Colorado Springs, we found ourselves reflecting on how far we had come over the years. Christin was back in school, smarter than ever, and piecing her life back together. (She is probably the only person I know who could go through major trauma, lose her memory, and be even more brilliant afterward.) And I—just coming off my second world championships where I swam all nine events on the program and won eight golds and one silver—was now a thirteen-time world champion only two and a half years after my paralysis. We both thought back to that night of Paralympic trials at the University of Minnesota.

"Remember when you looked to the pool deck and wondered if you could make it to Paralympic trials?" she asked me.

"Who would have thought this is where it would take me?" I replied.

"I knew you could do it!" she said with a grin. "Now, you aren't just hoping to make trials. You are fighting to become a Paralympic champion."

That was, of course, my dream, but there was something especially powerful about hearing my sister talk about it so frankly.

"Like I said that night," Christin added, "why not?"

———

The residential hall at the OTC was fairly basic—each apartment had two bedrooms and two baths, one on each side of a shared living room—but my roommate and I were determined to put our own flare into our suite. After all, that's what the IKEA furniture was for; plus, no one was here for the digs. This was the *Olympic Training Center*, and every athlete here had applied to live and train in preparation for the next Games. I had the added benefit of an internship with USA Swimming, which meant my time away from school wouldn't put me too many credits behind. The London Paralympics were just under two years away, and I was determined to maximize that time by making the OTC my home until we left for the United Kingdom.

Leaving my family and Chad and moving a thousand miles away felt as if I was sacrificing everything I loved in pursuit of my career, but I realized that sacrifice is all about perspective. I was choosing to seize the opportunities before me, even if it meant making the hard decisions along the way. I had to ask myself, "What am I doing today to bring myself toward where I want to be?" I wanted to become a Paralympic champion, and there were choices I had to make to get there. The truth is, it isn't a sacrifice if it points us in the direction of our dreams—it is a choice, a conscious decision. I didn't want to have a long-distance relationship with Chad or be away from my family, but I knew making decisions based on the emotions or convenience of the moment wouldn't bring me any closer to my long-term goals.

As much as I wanted to hit the water full bore the moment I arrived, I was determined to ease back into it after taking a few weeks off following Worlds—and what felt like a muscle strain in my back made that decision a lot easier for me to commit to. After two and a half years of pushing my body to the max every day, this was the first true break I'd had since I started swimming again three months after my paralysis; I didn't want to press my luck by diving back into workouts too quickly. That was what I told myself, anyway. In reality, I drew my sense of self from the extremes to which I could push my body. Without an intense training schedule, I hardly knew who I was. So I "eased" myself back in the pool following a schedule of what I pretended was a gentle ramp-up—and almost immediately realized my body was still hurting. I pressed stubbornly on, preparing relentlessly for an upcoming meet in California, less than a month away.

My mom flew out to stay with a friend who lived in the Bay Area and cheer me on at that meet in Palo Alto. The soreness in my back grew worse as the meet got closer, but I told myself all those stupid motivational phrases like "Pain is just weakness leaving the body" and "Today's pain is tomorrow's victory." Then, in the middle of my training session the day before the meet, I suddenly felt as if a knife had been plunged into the left side of my back, and I couldn't will my body to take one more stroke. By the time I returned to the hotel with the team, it had only gotten worse, and when I rushed to the bathroom in my room, I discovered I was peeing blood. You don't have to have a medical degree to know *that's not how that's supposed to work*. Shaking, I dialed my mom's cell phone, and she got in the car and rushed to the hotel to pick me up. An hour later we were at the Stanford Hospital ER, where I ended up spending four days battling a kidney infection. Then I flew home to Minnesota so my parents could help me while I recovered.

When I finally returned to the OTC in October, weeks later, I immediately resumed training despite the fact that I was still struggling with pain and vomiting every time I tried to eat. "It's just a complication from the kidney infection," I insisted anytime someone expressed concern. "I just need a little time to bounce back."

Chad came out for a visit to cheer me up. We spent the weekend in Vail, but thanks to the constant nausea, I could hardly leave my room. On our drive back to the OTC, he made an executive decision and took me to the ER and called my parents to tell them something was horribly wrong. With my mom on the next flight out, he flew home. This time the doctors discovered I had developed severe pancreatitis, which led to an extended hospital stay. The biggest challenge, however, wasn't the physical treatment; it was the emotional toll.

As the doctors prepared me for a simple procedure, they began to administer light sedation. But instead of calmly sinking into twilight like I was supposed to, the bright lights above in the procedure room, the sterile smell, and the steady beep of the heartbeat monitor triggered my deepest fears. Suddenly, I wasn't in Denver in the autumn of 2010; I was back in the clinic in January 2008. It was as if I knew what was coming but powerless to stop myself from being paralyzed all over again.

I began to sob uncontrollably and felt myself spiraling out of control, my mind and body in the grips of a full-fledged flashback. My reaction was so jarring that I required full sedation just so they could finish the procedure. This was my first medical emergency since my paralysis, and on a subconscious, almost primal level I couldn't help but connect the two experiences. But it wasn't over. My brain was still stuck in 2008. I was no longer experiencing the panic of a flashback; it was as if my mind had reset itself back to the day of my paralysis. In those first foggy few minutes, I didn't remember anything that had happened over the past two and a half years, which meant I had to be told all over again why

I couldn't feel the lower half of my body. I felt the overwhelming weight of my paralysis, and I gasped for air trying to come back to reality, attempting to bring my mind and heart back to the present, to 2010.

Over the next few weeks, my physical condition deteriorated, but I found strength in knowing that I wasn't alone—I had my mom, my sweet nurturing mother who slept on the cot in my room for two weeks. Throughout my time in the hospital, I underwent countless tests, more sleepless nights, and felt like a human pin cushion as IV lines blew out, causing veins to rupture. That ultimately led to getting a peripherally inserted central catheter (PICC) line to deliver medication, pain killers, and nutrition, since my body was rejecting everything we tried to put in my stomach. Physically, it was an excruciating few weeks—but my body was tough, and I knew it could weather any storm. Emotionally, I wasn't prepared for the flashbacks and the toll they took on my spirit.

My dad flew out to Colorado and drove my car home to Minnesota while my mom made plans to fly home with me so I could start my long road to recovery there. Again. My grand plan to live and train at the OTC for two years had not lasted even two months. Still, I was determined that I would defy every expectation and prognosis regarding my recovery time, and I would return to Colorado in the spring, ready to set my sights on London.

Unfortunately, my recovery was anything but straightforward. In January 2011, my gall bladder was removed, and I experienced yet another flashback in the hospital, evidence that moving on following trauma isn't an option; our trauma may always remain a part of us and resurface on its own time. As I lay at home with nothing to do except recover from the surgery, I was forced to face the harsh reality that my post-paralysis life was going to involve a whole lot more than just winning medals.

For the past three years, I had fixed my eyes on that black line at the bottom of the pool, pushing my body to see just how fast and strong I could become. I had not given my mind a chance to fully accept the reality of my paralysis before I rediscovered swimming, and from the moment I reentered the pool, I pushed myself to move forward—forward through the water, toward records, beyond grief.

Grief. That was the monster chasing me, the scary thing I thought I could get away from if I just kept moving. But just because I refused to look over my shoulder to stare it in the face didn't mean I wasn't carrying it through every stroke; just because I wouldn't acknowledge it didn't mean it went away. I had been so busy over the past three years that I had fooled myself into believing I was over the trauma—that I didn't need to mourn the life I had lost. I spent all my time hovering over a black line, convincing myself that each time I got faster, I regained more and more control over my past. I'd charged ahead, dead-set on convincing myself and everyone around me that I was going to be okay. I was so determined to prove to the world what my body could still do that I never gave myself a chance to be honest about what it couldn't. And the grief never left. It was always there, just waiting for the inevitable day when I couldn't outpace it anymore.

That was what frightened me most during my recovery. Why should I suddenly be having such an emotional response to something that happened to me so long ago, after so much life had happened in the interim? Shouldn't I be over it by now? Did the fact that I dove into my new life with so much vigor so quickly mean I had experienced grief all wrong? Did I walk away from walking again too soon? Had I made a mistake in allowing myself to embrace so much happiness so soon after something so devastating? Had I just spent the past three years living in denial?

As I tried to piece my body and my emotions back together, I struggled with the seeming contradictions between resilience and relapsing. All the work I'd invested in building a life for myself now seemed undone because of complications that are pretty typical for people with paraplegia and a couple of flashbacks in the hospital. So was I resilient or wasn't I?

During those slow, painful months of recovery, I came to realize that healing doesn't follow a prescribed timeline, and as much as I relished the illusion of control, I ultimately could not dictate exactly the way my life would play out. I could set goals and expectations, but I could not force the outcome. Healing isn't a one-and-done event. It's a process as unpredictable as life itself. As I eased myself back into the pool in the following weeks—*actually* taking it easy this time instead of just pretending to—I forced myself to consider what accepting this truth might look like for me.

———

I worked with Jimbo throughout spring 2011 to prepare for the Pan Pacific Para Swimming Championships. Our team trials were at the University of Minnesota in March, and I swam well enough not only to make the team for competition in August, but also to give myself the confidence I needed to trust my body. With that I began to realize one very important lesson: my body had not betrayed me, and rather than resenting its perceived imperfections, I needed to allow myself to celebrate its unwavering strength not only to adapt but to be the very vehicle to carry me toward my dreams. It gave me the strength to validate what I was beginning to suspect: as much as I loved the idea of living at the OTC, the training I was doing at home with Jimbo not only worked, but it was also the best thing for me. I could focus on my physical health and emotional well-being in a familiar environment surrounded by my loved ones. The moment I made the decision to move out of the OTC for good and base my training back in Minnesota, I felt like a huge burden had been lifted from my shoulders. I wasn't in limbo anymore, treating everything as temporary until I was well enough to return to the training center. I had resisted giving up on the OTC because it felt like it was one more step forward in my Great Big Plan; moving home (again) just felt like I was going backward. But that's because I was locked into thinking that healing could only move in one direction. So what if I was living with my parents once more if it was the best place for me to heal at that time? As long as I wasn't giving up, I was still making progress.

A few months after Pan Pac trials, my parents and I flew out to Colorado for the annual Jimi Flowers Classic swim meet in honor of the longtime Team USA coach who had recently passed away. Following the meet, we packed up my room for good. I tried to squeeze in a few "lasts" before I left the camaraderie of the training center, knowing that while returning home and training with Jimbo was best, it also meant I was going from a team environment to swimming predominantly one-on-one. I knew that sometimes we have to be willing to make the hard decisions between what we want in the moment and what we desire for our future.

On my final afternoon in Colorado, I was enjoying frozen yogurt with some teammates when my dad called my cell phone. I rolled away from the table for a minute to answer, and he told me in a voice that was clearly trying to stay calm: "Mal, an email just came through. Based on your performance at Worlds last year, you've been nominated for an ESPY."

Trying not to do my signature giddy screech, I put my phone down quietly, played it cool, and went back to talking with my teammates. I had no idea who the other nominees were, and I didn't want to make a big deal of my selection when any one of us could have been in the running. Still, I was completely freaking out on the inside. On one hand, I was ridiculously excited for the honor; on the other hand, I was nervous about the red carpet. Despite the progress I was making in how I viewed my body, the truth was that I still didn't love my reflection. I struggled to look in the mirror and believe that there was anything beautiful about the permanently seated woman looking back at me. Clothes fit differently when you're sitting as opposed to standing; they bunch up and hang in weird ways. I had pretty much given up on wearing dresses at that point because I couldn't feel comfortable in them. Short dresses put my legs on display—my atrophied, powerless legs. But long dresses were even worse because they covered my legs completely to the point that I felt disconnected from the lower part of my body. Since I no longer had sensation in my legs, the only way I could feel their presence was by seeing their outline through my pants; but with a full skirt covering up the visual reminder that my legs were still there, I felt like half of me was gone.

My mom and I headed to Neiman Marcus in Minneapolis almost as soon as we got home from Colorado, and dress shopping was every bit as terrible as I had feared. I hated how exposed I felt in anything short, and how incomplete I felt in anything long. I broke down crying over the sheer frustration of not being able to do something as simple as stand up to see how the dress looked on me. Finally, after several hours and a lot of tears, I found a knee-length, one-shoulder ivory dress with applique chiffon flowers running the length of the hem. As I turned in my chair, I realized I was grinning.

"Look at how it shows off my arms," I said to my mom.

"And your back looks stunning," she said, grinning as well.

For the first time in years, I felt glamorous, head-turning, and beautiful in my body, exactly the way it was.

But then, ten minutes later, dress paid for and hanging in its garment bag as we headed to the car, all those strong, beautiful feelings were erased as I stared at a four-inch curb I couldn't scale in my wheelchair. I felt broken and powerless again. Why couldn't I just appreciate my body for all it could do instead of resenting it for what it couldn't? What was wrong with me that I couldn't just celebrate the amazing career I was building? Why did I feel like an unstoppable Super Woman in the water but entirely surrounded by barriers on dry land? Why did every high have to get punctuated with a low? *And why couldn't I just get over it already—the emotional turmoil* and *the dumb curb?*

In the lead-up to the ESPYs, BMW came on as my first corporate sponsor, with a major announcement event planned for the end of July. I found myself in what felt like a game of emotional tug-of-war. There I was, beaming with pride over what I had accomplished just over three years following that horrific day: I was a thirteen-time world champion, fifteen-time world-record holder, an ESPY Award nominee, and I was signing on with my first corporate sponsor. Yet, in the background, I was still battling with the reality that I didn't have closure to the day I was paralyzed. I was still navigating the realities of what living life with a spinal cord injury meant, and I was struggling with the concept of allowing myself to truly move forward following tragedy—something that brought guilt.

As I experienced the entire spectrum of emotions at once that summer, I finally realized that I simply needed to *be*. I needed to allow myself to feel what I was feeling and not worry about whether it was somehow right or wrong. It was okay to feel pride in what my body could do while simultaneously mourning how it had changed without my consent. It was okay to get dressed up and feel like a princess while also getting mad that there was a step in front of me I couldn't scale. It's okay to feel whatever you are feeling, whenever you happen to feel it.

There's no such thing as "too soon" or "too long," provided that we are authentic about our emotions and don't hang out in either total victimhood or complete denial for the rest of our lives. One of the things that makes us human is our ability to experience more than one emotion at a time. It was okay that I felt the heights of joy and depths of loss; that didn't mean I was moving backward, and it didn't mean I was running away from my truth. It simply meant that I was a dynamic, complex, *real* human being who recognized nuance in life. I rolled into the ESPYs with a new appreciation for everything my body had done for me to get me to that point.

———

I will never forget the glare of the lights as I got out of the car to make my way down the red carpet at the Nokia Theater on July 13, 2011, for the ESPY Awards Ceremony. The whole experience felt like a dream: flying first class, staying at the swanky W Hotel in West Hollywood, two days of pre-parties where I got to hang out with athletes and celebrities whose names I'd only read in the headlines—Serena and Venus Williams, Kevin Love, Quinton Aaron. It was hard not to compare my experience now with the last time I had been in Los Angeles five years earlier, volunteering on Skid Row on my church's youth mission trip. Not only did the two experiences feel worlds apart, but in that five-year span, my entire world had changed—I was no longer walking down the streets of Los Angeles but rather wheeling. If anyone had tried to convince me back then that my life would take this direction, I never would have believed them. This was outside of anything I had ever considered.

My naivete was on full display the night of the awards. As Chad and I made our way down the red carpet, I was funneled off into an area backstage where a gentleman was standing, holding an ESPY. "It's my honor to congratulate you," he said, beaming.

I knew that some of the awards were not given onstage but rather recorded, so that the segments could be shown on the big screens to the audience during commercials or other breaks in the ceremony. But I figured that they taped all the nominees' reactions and then just played the winners' on the big screen inside when it was time to announce. I wanted to take a look at the trophy before I recorded my piece, thinking this might be my only chance to see an ESPY close-up. "Can I see it?" I asked, gesturing toward the ESPY.

The man gave me a strange look. "Of course."

I held the heavy award, turning it over in my hands and enjoying the weight of it. Suddenly, I gasped. "Wait, *my name's on there!*"

Everyone started to laugh. "That's why I said 'congratulations.'" The presenter grinned. "You won."

Wait, what? I'd just won an ESPY and I didn't even realize it? Oh my word, I felt like an idiot.

Don't lose focus, Mal, I said to myself. *You just won an ESPY!* Me. A woman who was an average varsity high school swimmer with two perfectly functional legs three and a half years ago was just named the Best Female Athlete with a Disability for 2011 by ESPN. What do I do now? Do I play it cool? Was that even possible at this point?

A few minutes later, I tried to call my parents, but my hands were shaking too badly to dial. Finally, I managed to hit all the numbers and Mom picked up: "We're at the Wolfgang Puck right down the street grabbing an appetizer," she chirped. "We'll be at the theater soon!"

"Cool," I replied. "Hey, have you guys ever seen an ESPY Award? No? Well, I'll show you mine after the show."

And, on cue, Chad texted them a photo of me holding up the statuette. Unlike me, they realized immediately that I had won and freaked out appropriately.

The show was an amazing experience for me down on the floor with the other nominees, but my mom and dad had almost as much fun being "Minnesota nice" and playing the proud parents up in the balcony, telling everyone within earshot that their daughter had just won an ESPY and striking up conversations with the people around them. They especially hit it off with a young man named Jay, who was sitting directly in front of them.

The next day, running on almost no sleep thanks to the after-party and the after-after-party, I packed up to head home and return to real life. As I was getting ready to leave, I realized there was no good way for me to transport my ten-pound, foot-and-a-half-tall ESPY without damaging it; it didn't come in any kind of a protective box and there was no way I was going to let it out of sight by checking it in my suitcase. Glancing around the room, I grabbed the only thing I could find that looked like it would make a halfway-decent carrier. And so, carrying my ESPY in the hotel pillowcase, I left for the airport.

"Ma'am, what is this?" a TSA agent asked an hour later, gesturing at the screen on the X-ray scanner. He peered closer. "It looks like an ESPY."

"It is," I said, grinning. "I won it last night."

The agent raised an eyebrow. "We're definitely going to have to swab it."

"Or you could just see it," I offered.

"That's cool, too," he replied. So I unwrapped the pillowcase and posed for some pictures with the TSA agents at LAX. It was amazing to see folks who encounter celebrities every day as a routine part of their jobs act like excited little kids when they spotted an ESPY.

Two weeks later, at the BMW Olympic sponsorship event celebrating one year to the London Games, I tried my hardest not to do the exact same thing as the TSA agents when I shared the stage with Janet Evans, one of my childhood heroes. Thankfully Chad was with me and helped me not be too much of a fangirl around her, but I know that was no easy task. I have to admit, though, I felt a little awkward when I noticed an extremely good-looking guy across the room. (We *definitely* locked eyes a few times.) I was happy in my relationship, and I kept Chad at my side that night. However, I couldn't help but feel beautiful when I thought about the handsome stranger who kept glancing my way. Even something as small as a couple of admiring glances boosted my confidence and reminded me that I didn't have to *walk* to feel pretty. Confidence is way more attractive than simply the ability to stand up. Strength is more beautiful than makeup and nice clothes—and people recognize that. Even hot guys at BMW events.

In August, I returned to Edmonton for the Pan Pac Championships, competing in nine races—seven individual events and two relays—and I took home gold in every single one. I even broke the world record in the 100-meter backstroke, the event in which I'd nabbed silver instead of gold by one-tenth of a second at Worlds the previous summer. That victory was particularly sweet. It was amazing to be back at the very pool where I broke my first world record in 2009 and see, yet again, just how much life had changed in a short period of time. While I was still grappling with emotions that had surfaced over the previous year, I also felt stronger than ever before. When we give ourselves permission to work through our emotional scars, we aren't admitting weakness; we are finding the power to meet ourselves where we are.

Representatives from a number of management agencies were reaching out to me now, and in the weeks following the championships, I pared down my list to a few contenders who aligned with my goals and ambitions. One of those happened to be The Factory Agency, the firm run by Jay, the guy my parents met at the ESPYs. When it turned out that he was going to be in Los Angeles at the same time my dad had an extended layover there for business, I asked if they would mind having a meeting.

After their breakfast together, Dad called me and said, "I really think Jay's your guy, Mal. His agency just feels like the right fit for what you've said you want to make of your career."

That settled it for me. I know it sounds crazy to sign with an agent I'd never met in person, but I trusted my dad's intuition and that there was a Great Plan at work. Something just felt serendipitous about the fact that this Jay guy had been sitting near my parents at the ESPYs, and they had already hit it off so well. I felt in my gut he was the one to go with, and part of this whole healing process was about regaining the confidence to trust myself—even if I knew I would still face moments of doubt and struggle down the road.

"Please send me the contract," I told Jay on our call following his meeting with my father, and I signed on with him and The Factory Agency at the end of September.

A month later, he flew to Minnesota so we could talk strategy for the lead-up to the London Games and finally meet face-to-face. I had just finished a lap during a particularly intense training session and was in the pool resting at the wall for a moment before I picked back up. The doors to the pool deck opened, and through my wet goggles, I could barely make out someone walking in. "Jay!" my dad called, waving him over. I wanted to say hello, so I lifted my goggles and then promptly snapped them right back on. The hot guy from the BMW event—the one I'd locked eyes with across the room—was my new agent.

Please, God, let me immediately melt into this water, I prayed. When I finally composed myself enough to get out of the pool and talk to him like a normal person, I agreed with my dad's assessment that Jay was a great guy and would represent me well, but I don't know when I have ever blushed so hard in all my life. I have never been so grateful for swim goggles so I could pretend to mess with them and buy a little extra time to pull myself together.

The corporate side of my career wasn't the only aspect that was taking off. I was ranked number one in the world in every event on the Paralympic program. Not only was I taking the swimming world by storm, but I suddenly found myself presented with a new avenue I had never considered before: public speaking. That September, my dad asked if I would be willing to "chat with a few folks" at his company's partner meeting in Baltimore later in the month. I took a deep breath and agreed; I knew many of his colleagues and thought a trip with my dad would be like the whole "Bring Your Daughter to Work Day" thing I always begged him to do when I was a kid.

About ten days before I left for the event, however, my dad broke the news that when he said I was invited to "chat with a few folks," it wasn't *quite* an accurate representation of what was truly happening. I was actually the keynote speaker with a ninety-minute slot.

"Are you serious, Dad?" I screeched. "What am I even supposed to talk about?"

"Just tell your story."

"*How?*"

My parents looked at each other. "Well, you did keep all those journals of your experience as you went through it."

In a huff, I scooted myself upstairs to my room above the garage at my parents' house, where I was currently living. I rooted under my bed until I found the box with all the journals that I had filled—page after anguished page—starting just a few days after my paralysis. At the time, all I was focused on was having an outlet for the mess of thoughts, feelings, reflections, and fears that were filling my brain. I never intended to revisit them. I think I believed that if I could only tear those thoughts out of my head and lock them away on the page, I'd be rid of those emotions forever. Now, sitting on the floor, I began to relive and remember a million things I had pretended to forget.

Several hours later, I emerged with the makings of a speech. It was rough and raw compared to the presentations I would give years down the road, but that very first keynote address was one of the most significant moments of healing after returning to the pool. It forced me to really explore the tangle of emotions that were impossible to process fully when I was first paralyzed, even if I had wanted to. There, spelled out in my own handwriting, were all my doubts of whether I would ever be able to build a life for myself. I confronted my anger that my body seemed to have betrayed me. I forced myself once again to face my fears that no one—including me—would ever fully love the new me. As I sat there on the floor—now a twenty-two-year-old with thirteen world championship medals, fifteen world records, and thirty American records—reading the words of a scared eighteen-year-old girl who had just lost the only way of life she ever knew, I realized how much I had changed. But just because I had come so far, it didn't mean the healing process was over; in fact, I realized it would probably never end. It would just keep changing and adapting along with me, taking on deeper meaning with every new experience and every new season of my life. And with every disappointment, setback, bad day, or major disaster waiting ahead for me, I would probably experience new pain that might compound the old. The pain might never fully go away. *And that's okay.*

There is no right or wrong way to mourn; there is only the path you take as you live in the midst of the experience. Even something you may think you are "over" is still a part of who you are; it still leaves its mark on your story and your heart. There's no such thing as leaving the past totally behind; life has a way of circling around, of doubling back, of taking unexpected detours to areas way off the map. True, the shortest line between two points is the most direct one, but that doesn't necessarily mean it's always the best. Sometimes there is a clear trigger for a setback in healing—like being in the hospital for the first major medical issue since my paralysis. Other times, that sadness, fear, or regret will hit you without rhyme, reason, or warning at 2:36 p.m. on a rainy Tuesday afternoon in the middle of September. The key to getting through it is to realize it's actually not a setback at all. It doesn't mean that anything is "wrong" with you or that you somehow didn't "do grief right" the first time around. It just means that you are a part of everything you have experienced, and everything you have experienced is a part of you. This is just one more step on the path toward where you ultimately want to be. Emotional healing isn't something you can chart on a predicable timeline. There are no "shoulds" when it comes to grief—there is just the reality of what you are feeling right now and where you want to be headed.

On that autumn afternoon in 2011, wiping tears from my eyes as I held those old journals in my hands, I knew that even though this was the first time I had dared to open them, it would not be the last. I needed to remember, not forget, in order to heal. My story is not a journey *to* healing, because I don't think it's a stopping point—but my journey *of* healing. Even now, when I regularly share my story without a second thought to auditoriums full of strangers, there is something healing in that, too—more than a decade after that first speech.

Healing isn't erasing what happened; it's moving forward with it. And my life *was* moving forward that fall. I had an amazing future in my sport, corporate sponsorships, and now (apparently) a speaking career—all things I didn't realize could be mine when I was first paralyzed. And just before Christmas, I got something else I had thought might never happen: an engagement ring and a fiancé. It was as if all my wildest dreams were coming true as I narrowed in on the London 2012 Games, and Chad and I began planning our wedding. Suddenly, everything seemed possible.

SIX

RISE ABOVE

There is a lightness in this moment, a freedom—for years I yearned for closure, believing that in order to move forward I had to hold the answers to what happened. However, I have come to find that closure doesn't come in the form of holding all the answers, but rather exists in a sense of being, in the lightness that comes when we release the burden of anger. As I spoke the words, "I forgive you," they didn't just roll off the tip of my tongue, but they were released from my heart—deeply aware that in that moment I created closure for myself, on my own terms.

—FROM PERSONAL JOURNAL, JANUARY 28, 2012

Setting a date. Booking a venue. Cake tasting. Flower arrangements. Color schemes. Dress shopping. The list grew and grew as we started planning our wedding for the following summer. On one hand, I didn't want to wait over a year to get married; on the other hand, it was rather daunting to consider planning the ceremony and reception while also training for the Paralympic Games. So, for now, I was content to be young and in love and admire the way my ring sparkled under the pool lights while I daydreamed of wedding details during training sessions.

Another date was looming even larger in my mind, though: the four-year anniversary of my paralysis. Four years may not seem like a particularly meaningful milestone, but this year was more than just a symbolic date; it marked the expiration of the statute of limitations for medical malpractice lawsuits in the state of Minnesota. In other words, I would no longer have open to me the option to bring a lawsuit against the hospital where I was paralyzed.

Within the first year of my paralysis, I decided I did not want to go down the road of litigation; it seemed draining, emotionally and physically exhausting, and, quite frankly, just not worth the damage it would do to my soul to have to relive the past, stirring up the trauma from that day and the anger associated with it. As the anniversary approached that would forever shut the door on that option, I did begin to waver a bit—not because I wanted to go through a lawsuit, but because I realized I would never get the answers I so desperately craved. I would never get clarity from the health-care system about what happened on January 21, 2008, and the days following. I would never be able to hear the doctors explain their actions both during and after the procedure. I would never find out exactly what happened in the procedure room. I would wake up to a wheelchair by my bedside for the rest of my days, never fully knowing the direct cause of my paralysis. And without answers to some of those basic, fundamental questions, how would I ever get closure?

As the reality of that date and all its implications sank in, I realized that the closure I so deeply desired came down to choosing to forgive. I poured my thoughts into my journal, processing my emotions as I wrote:

> It has been almost four years and I still don't have answers. I always thought of the things I would say if given the opportunity. For a while it was anger. I just wanted to scream, because it was so hard for me to understand why they didn't care to help me. I didn't understand how people could care more about their pride than doing the right thing. None of it made sense.
>
> Then the anger passed and I realized I couldn't hold on to my anger because it is a wasted emotion. Now I am more at the forgiving stage.

Then, on the morning of my fourth anniversary, I woke up to find my dad's letter—now an annual tradition—slid under my door. This one was a little different from the previous three, however. Instead of offering his own words, he chose to share messages he had received from countless individuals over the past year expressing how my story had offered them hope and sometimes even a way forward. Reading those words reminded me of the power of choice—choosing to rise above circumstance, anchoring ourselves to hope, and believing that good overcomes. I realized I had so much more to give to this world and to myself. As long as I lived with anger and resentment weighing on my heart, I would never fully find the freedom that comes with forgiveness. I looked at those familiar words at the bottom of Dad's letter—"You are the best, you can make a difference, and you can change the world"—and I realized this was my chance to change *my* world.

For the last year or two, I worked toward letting go of my anger, hurt, and resentment as I recognized that the cycle of hate and frustration had ruined my ability to trust people, to build healthy relationships, and to accept my new identity. My anger was only holding *me* back; it wasn't doing anything to affect the people who had hurt me. Nothing I might learn in a courtroom could change the fact that I was in a wheelchair permanently. Closure did not equal answers; it meant that I was letting go of the sense of loss they had caused me, and instead leaning into the fullness of the person I had become.

At my request, my parents reached out to the head of the medical system where I had been treated and explained the circumstances, and (to our surprise) they agreed to a face-to-face meeting with me.

Five days later, I met with them at their corporate offices downtown. As I set up a photo of myself in a frame—an eight-by-ten senior-year picture where I was standing upright and full of excitement about my life after high school—I read the journal I had written weeks prior, imagining this moment:

> If given the chance, I would tell them that I forgive them for taking a part of me that I can never get back. I forgive them for all the pain and suffering that they caused my family and me.

I forgive them for imprinting the image of me being paralyzed in my dad's eyes. I forgive them for the thud that I hear over and over again from when my legs dropped lifeless on the procedure table that day. I forgive them for the flashbacks I had for months of the very moment I was paralyzed. I forgive them for the years I went to bed and cried myself to sleep every night because it didn't make sense. I forgive them for the mornings when I wake up from a walking dream thinking I can walk only to fall straight to the floor. I forgive them for the confusion I have every morning I wake up and can't just get out of bed without having my chair there to remind me of the reality. I forgive them for the fact that I no longer remember what it feels like to stand on my own two feet. I forgive them for those days when winter turns to spring and all I want to do is go for a run and I can't. I forgive them for taking away the moment when I get married and being able to walk arm in arm down the aisle with my dad. I forgive them for what my children will go through. I forgive them for the fact that I won't be able to teach my kids how to ride a bike or kick a soccer ball. I forgive them for all of the pain I have when I sit on the ground and crawl up and down the stairs in my home every day. I forgive them for the fact that I can't feel the sand between my toes anymore, for the fact that I can't just take a walk on the beach. I forgive them for everything.

As I shared my words of forgiveness in that room, I felt myself take back control, releasing the hurt that was so deeply buried within my soul, saying the words that I needed to articulate out loud: "I forgive everyone involved in what happened that day and the days following." As I wheeled out of the building, I felt heard and seen, but more importantly, I felt free. There was nothing I needed from them. I didn't need an explanation of exactly what happened that day—not anymore. Letting go was no longer dependent on understanding the how but in finding peace with who I had become since January 21, 2008. In the act of forgiveness, I created my own closure—and most of all, I reclaimed my power.

In my journey toward healing, I found that forgiveness is the way we liberate ourselves as we let go of anger, resentment, and hate, and instead fill our hearts with love, compassion, and hope. There is a power that comes with forgiveness—a lightness of spirit. For years I didn't believe that the health-care system deserved my forgiveness, but I finally realized that *I* deserved to forgive. What happened to me on January 21, 2008, and everything that followed brought enough hurt for a lifetime—not just for myself, but for those involved who may have carried guilt or pain. While I couldn't control the events of that day, I *could* choose to release everyone involved by letting them know I was not broken by that moment.

The day after that meeting, I dove into the pool and felt faster than ever before. It was as if invisible shackles I hadn't even realized were there had finally been broken, and nothing—not my body, my mind, my emotions, my fears, my insecurities, or my past—*nothing* was holding me back.

That spring, my career continued to climb. In March, I signed on with my fourth sponsor, Proctor and Gamble (P&G), as part of their "Thank you, Mom" campaign, in which Olympians and Paralympians paid special tribute to the women who raised us and encouraged us as we pursued our athletic dreams. The following month, I made several trips for P&G as well as a visit to Los Angeles for a BMW event to mark one hundred days from the start of the Games. As Mom, Dad, Jay, and I crisscrossed the country, I began to realize how much was involved with the *business* side of professional sports. I watched as other athletes went from one interview to the next or attended events with their sponsors. I watched as Jay worked exhaustlessly for his clients, building relationships, working on partnerships, and advocating for their voices to be heard in corporate conversations.

The broader world of professional sports was opening up to me, and I was eager to learn more, since it looked like I might be a part of those conversations following London too. I was either the reigning world champion or the current world-record holder in all seven individual events in which I was slated to compete. Provided I didn't let my success go to my head and continued training as hard as I could, I was anticipating a very successful performance and several appearances on the medal podium.

But as I entered the final push of training leading into trials, I got a nagging feeling that something in my life was still not exactly as it should be. Despite rejecting other people's limits on my life and committing to forgiveness, something still seemed misaligned, like a favorite shirt that doesn't *quite* fit right anymore. And suddenly, I found that the wedding plans and future vision of myself that I had been so excited about just a few months ago began to feel . . . off. I loved my fiancé and I wanted us to build a family, but suddenly the path we'd planned didn't seem quite so clear, obvious, or natural. The person Chad fell in love with two years ago was someone else—a twenty-one-year-old just emerging from a life-altering trauma and relearning who she was all over again. I wasn't that person anymore. We had both grown during our time together, but now I could see that we had grown in two very different directions.

After a lot of agonizing conversations, I reluctantly took off my ring and asked Chad to hold it for me until after London. I didn't want to call off the engagement, but I couldn't afford to be distracted by worries, questions, and petty arguments while I was focusing on trials and, ultimately, the Games. "We will work this out afterward," we agreed, and I felt confident we would.

Before I knew it, the Paralympic trials in Bismarck, North Dakota, were upon us, and the challenges in my personal life still spilled over into my performance in the water. My first race was admittedly a disaster; Jimbo pulled me aside that morning and told me I needed to refocus. I went back to the hotel that afternoon and took the time between prelims and finals to recenter myself. I reflected on my journey to that moment—to the brink of being named to Team USA—and realized I owed it to myself to drown out all my other concerns and focus entirely on my swimming. It wasn't selfishness; it was recognizing that the incredible opportunity I had worked for might slip away if I didn't get my head where it needed to be. I went back to the pool that night for finals a different swimmer, and I conquered the weekend, sweeping all my events and breaking a long-sought-after world record in the 50-meter butterfly. Next thing I knew, three days of racing had passed, and I was sitting in a conference room with my parents at my side as I heard my name called as a member of Team USA for the London 2012 Paralympic Games.

In July I received notice that my classification would be reviewed when I reached London. As I mentioned, in the Paralympic movement, each athlete is classed based on his or her physical impairment for the sake of parity in competition. A medical team scores your entire body on a point system, and the total places you on a sliding scale that determines your classification. S7, the class in which I competed, includes individuals who have half of their body affected by cerebral palsy or other neurological conditions, individuals who have dwarfism, and individuals with spinal cord injuries, just to name a few. Although the impairments vary, the manner in which each body functions as a whole is similar. Because I am a complete paraplegic, I figured this was a simple technicality; being moved to a different class didn't even seem in the realm of possibility.

In August, a few weeks prior to the start of competition, my teammates and I made our way to the American army base in Stuttgart, Germany, for our final training preparations. While there, I had time not only to fine-tune my training but also to reflect. One evening, I took some time for myself to flip through a book my parents compiled for me before I left. It was filled with letters of encouragement from every corner of our world: former teammates, colleagues of my parents, family members, friends, and neighbors. As I sat in my room that night, I knew that whatever happened in the coming days, I wasn't alone.

Along with a few of the other swimmers who were also up for review, I left the team training camp early and made my way to London for my classification appointment. That day, I held on to an unwavering faith that while the appointment would be difficult—strangers assessing all that my body was no longer capable of—when I emerged, I would have no worries other than the start of competition.

I was wrong.

When the review committee came back with the evaluations, I learned that I had been reclassified. Despite the fact that I have zero function below my waist because of damage to my spinal cord, my classification was changed to S8: "Swimmers who have lost either both hands or one arm [or] athletes with severe restrictions in the joints of the lower limbs." In other words, I suddenly found myself up against athletes with vastly more physical movement and control of their bodies. Going into the London Games as an S7, I was projected to sweep gold in all nine events—seven individual races and two relays; now, as an S8, I would be swimming in fewer events, and it seemed unlikely I would reach the podium at all. In an instant, it felt as if everything I had worked for and all the personal progress I had made had been torn from me. It wasn't just that I had been moved to a tougher class just seventy-two hours before I was supposed to compete on the biggest stage of my life, but that one decision brought years of trauma back to the surface.

For a moment, I sat silently on the London Aquatics Centre pool deck—the same place that had been the background on my computer for the past six months, the spot I had been dreaming of—and I felt the breath had just been knocked out of my lungs. With some swimmers doing warm-ups in the water and others filing onto the pool deck to begin, I felt incredibly self-conscious and exposed. Quickly, I grabbed my bag and wheeled myself out of the public area to the hallway lined with several accessible, self-contained bathroom stalls. Slipping into one, I locked the door behind me with shaking hands and began to sob—gut-wrenching, heartbreaking cries. Everything I had dared to dream for myself, everything I had chased for the past four years seemed as if it had all been snatched from me in an instant.

When I recovered myself enough to form words, I called my parents' cell phone to let them know that there would be a change of plans when they arrived in London.

"What's up, honey?" Mom asked when she heard my voice. "We're on the train from Paris to London right now."

"We're packing my bags when you get here and going home," I announced, breaking down in tears all over again as I explained what happened.

"Just let us get there and we will come up with a plan," Dad said. "Don't give up."

Meanwhile, my coaches were scrambling to file an appeal, with Jay assisting them however he could. Maybe, just maybe, there was a chance the decision would be reversed. The morning of opening ceremonies, a representative from Team USA fetched me from my room in the Paralympic Village to take me to our team's administrative offices. The moment I rolled into the room, I knew from the somber atmosphere that the appeal had been denied.

Afterward, I called my parents again—families are not allowed in the athletes' village, so I couldn't relay anything in person—and informed them I would not be swimming the S7 100-meter backstroke the next morning as we'd hoped. I would definitely be an S8 in the six individual events I was now competing, which meant they faced the challenge of trying to locate tickets for different events than they'd planned. Since most events were sold out, this proved a momentous task, but I just had to trust that it would work out. I needed to focus my attention on getting ready for a whole new competition.

I began furiously researching the other swimmers in my new class. What kinds of times were they posting? Who had the best mental game? Who swam better in finals versus prelims and who swam slower under pressure? As I read up on the incredible women I would be facing, it was hard not to feel intimidated, especially since I would be the only one in my races who was not able to walk to the starting blocks.

Thankfully, Jimbo snapped me out of the panic spiral. "You're allowed to be upset, but you can't feel so sorry for yourself that you don't get your head in the game," he told me.

My parents gave me a gentler nudge. "Go to opening ceremonies tonight and enjoy the moment. You worked too hard to get here to allow this to take that from you."

They were right, and I knew it. I couldn't allow my circumstances to control me, and I shouldn't hand over the reins of my destiny to disappointment. I quickly learned that trying to understand the reason I was moved into a different classification ultimately didn't matter; while I couldn't change the ruling, the ruling couldn't change the fact that I was at the Paralympic Games. I had a job to do and a dream to chase.

That night, as we lined up for the Parade of Nations, I still felt numb. The United States of America was obviously at the far back of the alphabetical line, and as we made our way from the village to the Olympic stadium, I struggled to find the joy I so desperately wanted to feel. At the tunnel, as we prepared to make our entrance, someone began shouting "U-S-A! U-S-A!" We all took up the chant, and the noise seemed to fill the dark space. When I got closer to the bright mouth of the tunnel, the lights, color, and cheers of the stadium rushed forward to meet us and filled my senses with all the celebration, hope, and excitement I had temporarily lost sight of. No matter what happened in the pool, I would return home at the end of the Games a Paralympian, and no one could ever take that from me. The terrified teenager who had leaned over the railing at the University of Minnesota pool and said "Maybe in four years I could be there" had longed to make an appearance at trials. Now here I was, not just at trials but about to wave to the crowd as a member of Team USA. I had already gone further than I dared dream.

As I exited the tunnel into the full roar of the stadium, I was determined in that moment that I would rise above. My story was never about what happened to me; it was always about what I did with it. Why should I change that now?

My first race two days later was a qualified success. I made finals, but I finished in the middle of the pack. The podium was still just a dream. I fixed my sights on the 50-meter freestyle on September 2, and I secured the fifth-fastest time in prelims. A few hours later, moments before I checked in to the ready room for finals, I put on my headphones and blasted my favorite go-to pre-race song, "All I Do Is Win" by DJ Khaled. Just then, I felt a hand lift one side of my headphones. Fellow Team USA swimmer Joe Wise leaned in and said one simple sentence: "Go shock the world." Those were the last words anyone spoke to me that evening before my race. Before I knew it, the required twenty minutes in the ready room had passed, and we were preparing to be called out for our race. With those words and "All I Do Is Win" playing on a loop, I rolled out onto the pool deck as my name was announced.

Those sounds were still echoing in my head as I removed my Team USA jacket and headphones and pulled myself onto the starting block. Just before snapping my goggles into place, I stared down the black line of lane two, and everything went silent. I couldn't look for my family since they were scattered all over the stands, wherever they had managed to find available tickets, but I felt them all at my back. In fact, I felt my entire community at my back—everyone who had been a part of my story, a part of getting me to this moment—behind me, pushing me forward and spurring me on. I took a deep breath, filling my lungs with not just air but hope, confidence, and love—so much love. Then, as the horn sounded, I dove in.

It was a perfect start; I could tell that the moment I hit the water. I immediately began placing one hand in front of the other as I formed freestyle strokes, and with each stroke I felt increasingly powerful. At the 25-meter mark, I took my one and only breath of the entire race; tilting my head to my left side, I saw only the feet of the swimmer in lane three. Instantly, I realized I only had 25 meters to make up an entire body length, which didn't seem like enough time at all. But instead of panicking, my mind and body seemed to know what to do, and I felt myself seized by one thought: *It's never too late to fight for what you want.* So I pushed forward, determined not to slow down until my hand touched the wall. Seconds later, I made the final reach and finished, oblivious to everything else around me. I was already smiling by the time I grabbed the edge of the pool to pull myself up. I had no idea where I finished, but I knew that everything I had gone through over the past four and a half years had led to this moment—I had swum in a Paralympic final. Rising to the surface, I noticed a single light on the starting block, denoting first place. Not believing my eyes, I turned around to check the scoreboard only to see my face on the jumbotron and hear the announcer shout, "Mallory Weggemann takes the gold medal and a new Paralympic record!"

There it was: 31.13 seconds. I turned back to the wall and dropped my head for just a moment while I laughed in disbelief. Then I turned back around and smiled, waving to my family, wherever they were, as my teammate Jessica Long dove across two lanes to wrap me in a massive hug.

A few minutes later, I made my way down the media line. "I've dreamed of this moment for four and a half years," I said, leaning into a microphone. "I came in here wanting to win gold. When I was reclassed, I decided I still wanted a gold medal. And to be able to go out there tonight and do just that was absolutely amazing."

Somehow, my dad managed to weave his way through the crowd to get close and snapped a photo of me as I wheeled off the deck, grinning at him and holding up my index finger to show "number one." As I entered the hallway that led back to the locker rooms, I found myself fumbling for my phone and automatically dialing someone I didn't even fully register until his voice greeted me on the other line.

"*Are you kidding me?* That was amazing! How does it feel to be a Paralympic gold medalist?" Jay gushed as he answered. I was surprised to hear him, but we chatted for just a minute before I had to go. Despite everything I was already feeling, I suddenly felt a new emotion too. In the midst of the biggest accomplishment of my life, Jay was the one person I wanted to talk to.

A few minutes later, as I took the medal stand and lowered my head, the weight of the medal surprised me in all the best ways. It was heavy, but not in a way that felt like a burden; it was more a sense of substance and gravitas, the weight of experience and victory. My family, Jimbo, and Jay—finally all together in one place—stood to my right. To my left were my teammates. The community of people who had filled my life with color and refused to give up on me when I wanted to give up on myself were all a part of this moment. I was surrounded by people who showed me how to rise above even the worst disappointments and setbacks when I couldn't imagine how it was possible. We are only as good as the people we surround ourselves with, and I knew I was surrounded by the very best.

As the flag rose and the anthem began to play, I couldn't help but be struck by the incredible symbolism of it all: complete heartbreak turned into a beautiful victory. My Paralympic journey matched my personal journey: choosing to rise above despite the circumstances; hope helping me see that regardless of how dark the days feel, there is brightness on the horizon; love encompassing me, reminding me I am never alone; faith anchoring me in a deep-rooted belief that good always overcomes; resilience giving me the strength to show up and fight another day. In that moment, I felt four years come full circle.

I did a handful of interviews following the medal ceremony, and through them all, I couldn't shake the awareness that I was there because of everyone who loved me pulling together to propel me forward. "Just to be up there and see that flag raised and hear the national anthem and hear our team chanting USA . . . nothing compares to that," I told one reporter. "It was like everything that has happened . . . all the hard work, and the tears, joy, and everything that's gone into this, my family and all the supporters I've had, I just saw that journey come together, and I got my dream."

But there was one other major hurdle I needed to navigate. Amid the celebrations and excitement of London, I recognized that I was lying to myself about my engagement. The challenges Chad and I had were bigger than a postponement; no matter how badly I wanted to make things work, sometimes they simply aren't meant to be. After my initial shock of reclassification, I knew in my bones that I was supposed to stay in the fight; in doing so, I rose above the disappointment, anger, and frustration. But rising above doesn't always mean sticking it out; it simply means doing the right thing and trusting that everything will work out. I knew in my heart of hearts that my engagement needed to end—that what was broken between us wasn't something that could be fixed with time. I knew I had to do what needed to be done, and I simply had to hold on to the faith that it would work out in the end.

In swimming, as in life, there are things that can pull us down, weights we may not even be aware of until we let go. By letting go of the desire for justice when I faced those medical executives, my life and future became my own. My forgiveness wasn't for them; it was for *me*, so *I* could find the freedom on the other side of my anger. I wasn't even aware of how heavy a burden I had been carrying until I released it. By letting go of the hurt of my reclassification, I found that my victories were even sweeter. I didn't let circumstances outside my control become the forces that dictated my story, but instead allowed my strength to propel me to the top. By letting go of my engagement, I acknowledged the power of healing to restore my heart so I could grow into the fullness of who I had become, instead of staying tethered to ideas of who I used to be.

I left London with a gold in the 50-meter freestyle, a bronze in the 4×100 medley relay, and a new understanding of what it takes to pull strength from yourself and lean on others when you feel completely and utterly defeated. I realized the importance of trusting myself to find a way to rise in any situation—to react with dignity, strength, and truth. It's our responses, not our circumstances, that define us in the end. Our lives reflect the choices we make with the hand we are dealt, not the cards themselves. It's up to each of us to decide whether to keep fighting and rise above all that seeks to keep us down or give up and accept the weights and challenges that constrain us.

Whatever burdens you are carrying in your life, know that you inherently possess the power to rise above them. In the water, your body instinctively wants to find air. Lose the things that are keeping you below water and allow yourself to surface. Allow yourself the freedom of breathing again—that's what keeps you alive. The weight of anger, resentment, and regret only weigh down the person still carrying them; in other words, holding on to resentment doesn't hurt anyone but you. Let those burdens go and let your soul rise above.

Forgiveness is one of the hardest obstacles you will ever face, but it's also one of the most rewarding, because *you* are the person who benefits most. It doesn't matter that I may never again see the doctors who treated me; the forgiveness was for me, not for them. It doesn't matter if my classification was challenged by someone else; it didn't stop me from knowing the truth of who I am.

Whatever challenges you may be facing in your own life, chances are there are burdens you carry along with them. I encourage you to look honestly at the things holding you back—old grudges, blame, or resentment—and decide if they are worth it. Is holding on to anger worth the toll it takes on your soul? Is throwing in the towel because of a disappointing call that didn't go your way worth the shot at your dreams? Whether you are faced with forgiving people for their actions or deciding to press forward beyond an upsetting situation, the choice is yours to either sink into bitterness or rise above. Only one of those options offers any real change; only one of them takes you to the freedom of the surface. When we choose to rise above, we are the ones who come out on top, who find freedom, who emerge stronger and more resilient.

SEVEN

FIND YOUR WHY

Tomorrow is my day to celebrate life and everything that it has to offer, because although I had something taken from me five years ago tomorrow, they didn't strip me of my ability to live.

—FROM PERSONAL JOURNAL, JANUARY 20, 2013

Now what?

That was the question that haunted me in the fall of 2012. I'd been warned by countless experienced athletes that the post-Games slump was a real thing, but that seemed impossible. How could anyone feel directionless or uninspired after an experience as incredible as the Paralympics? I was certain I was going to be riding that high forever.

Yet here I was, two months later, sitting in my room and staring at my two hard-fought medals as I asked myself that question over and over.

The weeks since London were an absolute whirlwind. The closing ceremony was September 9, with Coldplay, Jay-Z, Rihanna, and the British Paraorchestra performing at the Olympic stadium. I kept thinking back to that night, surrounded by my teammates. Not only did I feel the world come together as we all celebrated the closing of the 2012 Paralympic Games, but *my* world came together. I had a moment of clarity, when everything that happened over the past four and a half years all made sense. In so many ways, London seemed like the close of the first chapter of my life with paralysis and the launch into the next phase of who I was meant to be.

My family flew home to Minnesota while Jay and I made our way to Washington, DC, for the Team USA visit to the White House on September 14. As we gathered on the front lawn with President Obama and the First Lady, I realized that what I had just done in London was so much larger than myself; unfortunately, I wasn't exactly sure what that was. I felt more anchored and grounded in my story than ever before—but the nagging questions that were already beginning to form in the back of my mind started to drown out everything else: "But *why* did you do all this? *Now what?*" As long as the celebrations continued, however, I could push those thoughts away.

Thankfully, the celebrations *did* continue. Christin always spearheads the efforts to have grand "Welcome home!" decorations waiting to greet me when I pull in to the driveway after a meet; this time, she had dozens of #1 and American flag balloons, along with trays of cookies decorated to look like gold medals. But the real celebration came a few days later when my parents threw a massive party at their house and invited everyone who had been a part of my recovery and support community. Friends from church who helped build my first ramp; members of my high school swim team and our coach, Steve; Roxanne, who lent me her suit that very first practice back in 2008; Jay, who was no longer just my business manager but also a dear friend; old neighbors; new friends; extended family—it seemed like anyone and everyone who had helped shape me into who I was or touched my story in some way was there to celebrate with me.

But now the excitement and immediacy of all of that was over, and it was back to life as usual—except, what did "as usual" mean anymore? In the span of four and a half years, I had gone from being paralyzed to making it my sole purpose to train for the Paralympics, to actually competing in the Games, to . . . *now what?* There it was again, the question I couldn't answer and couldn't ignore. My sport had given me an identity for the present and hope for a future when I needed it most, but I couldn't live my life in the pool. On the other side of the Paralympics, I had to figure out who I was on dry land.

I knew all too well that I wasn't living any version of the life I had planned for myself just a matter of months ago. Turning to my journals to sort out my thoughts, I worked through a lot of my struggles on paper. I wrote:

Lately I have been thinking a lot about life and the plans that we have for ourselves. Truth is, those often differ from the plans that life has in store. Six months ago, I had it all mapped out. I was going to come home from London as the most decorated athlete of these Games. I was going to have nine gold medals and everything I had worked for would have paid off in that very moment. I was going to have a wedding to plan. It was going to be a dream come true, my happy ending, and then life happened. Now, I am sitting here with one gold medal, one bronze medal and an empty ring finger.

I was seeking balance—to embrace the present while not getting lost in the uncertainty that lay ahead. Thankfully, a number of exciting opportunities came my way that fall. I did several more press interviews and continued my speaking career. I even got to try my hand at professional writing when CNN.com asked me to compose a series of opinion pieces. One in particular was about the lack of American media coverage of the Paralympics, despite our events selling 2.7 million tickets and garnering extensive attention elsewhere in the world. I did so gladly, happy to use my interest in journalism to give a voice to a movement that mattered deeply to me. But even while I was embracing new opportunities, I didn't feel that my goals had any direction. I had ideas and ambitions, sure. But a road map? No chance. I had just gone from planning my life in a four-year segment—from watching the trials for Beijing in 2008 to competing in London in 2012—to . . . what?

I found myself searching for answers to that nagging question of *now what?* Personally, my life felt messy at best. I had gone from planning a wedding to calling off an engagement. Truth be told, it felt as if I was letting people down. We all feel social pressure regarding the way things are "supposed" to happen in a relation-ship: date, fall in love, get engaged, and then get married. Once Chad and I got engaged, I felt obligated to follow in lockstep, even though my heart was telling me otherwise, because getting mar-ried was what I was *supposed* to do. I loved him deeply, but with time, I found I simply wasn't *in* love with him anymore. We had grown apart, and I felt lost and alone instead of supported and fulfilled with him. But I still felt like getting married was expected of me, so I convinced myself to ignore my heart. It wasn't until that night in London, when I reached for my phone to call Jay after my 50-meter freestyle, moments after breaking the Paralympic record, that I realized I owed it to myself to listen to my heart and honor my truth, no matter how messy it may be.

I found myself trying to make sense of not only the last few months but my journey over the last four years. I knew I wanted to train for another Games, but I also felt a burning desire to find my deeper purpose. Despite closing in on nearly five years since my paralysis, I still longed for an answer to that underlying question: Why was I paralyzed? If I truly believed that everything happens for a reason, there must have been a reason for January 21, 2008, too. Then, in November, I caught my first glimpse of an answer to that intimate, even spiritual question of *why*.

My parents learned about a young woman in the Twin Cities named Kelsey who had been paralyzed over the summer and asked if I would be willing to pay her a visit. A week later, I took a deep breath and wheeled myself through the doors of her rehab facility—the first time I had been in such a facility since I was a patient myself. Even though it wasn't the same hospital, I was worried the setting would be triggering for me, but I also knew I couldn't let my fears control my life. I brought my medals to show Kelsey, and we talked about her injury, her fears, her goals, and what life in a wheelchair did—and did not—look like. We also hit on the seemingly trivial but legitimately important questions, like what type of shoes you could wear following paralysis. Reality is, after paralysis, what once used to seem small is momentous— *nothing* feels simple anymore. I yearned to have someone to look to following my injury, to see a path forward. That void motivated me to be a beacon for others, even if it was just showing them possibilities of footwear.

That day, I was rocking a pair of knee-high leather boots with beautiful block heels—a post-London gift to myself. As Kelsey sat in her chair with a pair of socks on her feet and various bedroom slippers by her bedside, she looked at me with a spark in her eyes and gasped, "You can still wear heels?!" I assured her that I actually did on every possible occasion. Not every question surrounding trauma has to pack earthshaking significance; sometimes, yearning for something as simple as pretty shoes is a comforting reminder that life goes on.

By the time I left the rehab center, I realized I had turned a corner in my own journey. Not only did I feel the freedom that comes with forgiveness, but I also understood that having gone through that process, I was now able to reach out to others to offer comfort and care that I couldn't before coming to terms with my own grief. I wanted to give Kelsey the hope and encouragement that my family and I had craved so desperately during those diffi-cult early months. The unanswered questions had left holes in my own life, and it wasn't until I created my own closure that I could fill in those holes with resilience and hope—and then turn my energy outward to help other people do the same.

After all, I had been living with a wheelchair for nearly five years; I was no longer a "newly paralyzed" person. I had a responsibility to connect with other people facing challenges of their own, to give them hope and remind them of their inherent worth. Just like that, the underlying question of *why* that weighed so heavily on my heart began to fade. All it took was that visit with Kelsey to show me that if I could offer someone hope, maybe that was enough to give my own journey a deeper meaning. My dad's bedtime mantra echoed in my head; we all really do have the power to change the world. Simply by shifting our own outlook, we change our own little corner of the planet, and that ripples outward.

By the time 2012 came to a close, I realized that my insight into *why* enabled me to let go of the nagging question of *now what?* I had to give myself permission to accept that it is okay not to have every answer; it is okay to paint on a blank canvas one color at a time and not live by a clearly dictated timeline drawn out four years in advance. Sometimes, it is okay to just *be*. When I took a step back and thought about everything the past year had shown me, I found my greatest pride didn't lie in the singular moment of becoming a Paralympic gold medalist, but rather in discovering the power of forgiveness and the depth of my own worth, which gave me the courage to follow my heart and let go of something good in order to pursue something great.

As the five-year anniversary of my paralysis approached, I wanted to continue to choose joy on the other side of loss. My parents, Jay, and I went to Mammoth Mountain in California so I could try monoskiing (adaptive downhill skiing). We dedicated our first full day to getting a feel for the mountain and learning the basics with an instructor, but by day two, we were adventuring all over the mountain. I loved the freedom that came with skiing—that everywhere I turned, I had the power to create fresh tracks and a path of my own choosing. In my journal that night, I marveled at the lack of restraint I felt as I tore down the slopes:

> In that moment I felt truly alive. I was skiing down a mountain and I was free in every sense of the word. I was free from the anger I held on to for so long, I was free from the fear of what this meant for my life, I was free from the uncertainty, I was free from "what ifs" and "why me's." I was in a place of pure joy and happiness for where I am at in life, and most of all, I was in a place where I felt love. Love for myself, love for the things that I am passionate about, and love for life.

My parents felt the significance of my anniversary too. That annual observation wasn't just about my own healing; it was also about my parents healing their own trauma of watching their child's life change so drastically. Our yearly celebrations became a tradition that we marked together without fail. As we collectively celebrated that year at Mammoth Mountain, my mom gave me a card where she reminded me yet again that good really does overcome. And my dad, in his annual letter to me, wrote: "Reflect on the ripples. You have been given a gift; you have been given the ability to affect people and motivate them. It is my prayer that your life will be filled with love, that you will continue to send ripples of hope throughout this world."

As 2013 took shape, I realized that I had found the most important part of my identity. I sat atop the mountain before my final run of the weekend, and as I took a deep breath, I knew that not only was I going to be okay, I was truly at peace. My value wasn't determined by records or accolades, and it wasn't rooted in my trauma. My value was defined by the person I had chosen to become. I had the chance to lean into that identity and explore the tremendous gift it really was.

When I first returned to the pool following my paralysis, swimming saved my life by giving me purpose again. So, that spring, when I was invited to be part of a documentary called *The Current*, about the healing power of water, I didn't think twice about accepting. The film featured surfer and shark-attack survivor Bethany Hamilton, Olympic gold medalist Missy Franklin, and me. Amazingly, this meant that my whole family was invited to spend a week diving and snorkeling in Bimini, in the Bahamas, as the filmmakers took footage of us in the ocean.

Apart from the water, the trip still had healing properties for my family, since we realized that this would be the first time since Christin had gotten sick—more than ten years ago—that the five of us were able to go on vacation together. I celebrated my twenty-fourth birthday there, surrounded by my family and Jay. While Jay and I had worked together for the past year and a half, he now joined me on that trip not as my manager but as my boyfriend. Over the course of the six months after London, I yearned to know what my path forward looked like, but I failed to realize that each day I was already living it. I found the final pieces of closure to the trauma of my past: I was mending the heartbreak of watching my engagement fall apart while realizing that fate was bringing Jay and me together. As we celebrated my birthday on our first night in Bimini, under the thatched roof of the quaint restaurant at the small marina game club where we were all staying, our table was filled with love. The sounds of laughter showed me that my family and I had made it through the past decade together, and we even expanded our circle along the way.

Each day in Bimini, my family, Missy Franklin's family, the film crew, and the captain loaded onto the dive boat. Our days on the boat were filled with dropping in for dives and cruising the vast blue waters as I put my scuba certification to use for the first time since my paralysis. From time to time, we spotted pods of dolphins. The captain allowed Missy and me to ease carefully into the water alongside them. We took a scarf with us to drop, and watched as the dolphins brought it back up to the surface and waited eagerly for us to toss it again. Every day brought moments that took my breath away; every evening filled with that same joyful laughter that crowded around the dinner table that first night.

The production crew also treated me to a side trip of special significance. The day of my paralysis also happened to be Martin Luther King Jr. Day, and ever since, I felt a strong connection to a man who displayed such profound courage and bravery in the face of overwhelming social pressure to give up. The team knew this aspect of my story, and one afternoon, we waited to time the tide just right so we could get the boat through the waters to the same mangroves that had been one of Dr. King's favorite retreats— the spot where he stepped away from the busyness of life to pen his Nobel Peace Prize acceptance speech. I found myself sitting in the stillness of the mangroves as I reflected on my own journey of healing, deeply aware of the profound historical significance of the land. Even though our struggles were completely different, I found comfort and inspiration in his writings; while he faced overwhelming odds and incredible challenges, he still seized life and inspired the world with a message of hope and empowerment, and the challenge to value love over bitterness.

That spring, I continued to explore my identity outside of competitive swimming—one rooted in who I was, not what I could accomplish. I'd spent years hovering over a black line, chasing the ultimate dream of Paralympic gold; now, I found myself peeling back the layers to discover the person whom this pursuit had helped shape. Being laser focused on my goals had guided me through my first few years of paralysis, but now I could meet the new me for the first time—the person I'd become on the other side of trauma, the me who was resting under the surface of my newfound success. I was no longer a young girl who had *suffered* a spinal cord injury, but a young woman who was living and thriving *with* a spinal cord injury.

Nothing drove that point home to me more than when, a few months later, I received an unexpected invitation to speak in front of the General Assembly chamber at the United Nations in New York for a TEDx event in September. The theme of the event was "Brave: United in Action," and for ten minutes I would have the opportunity to speak about what bravery meant to me. I would have the power to leave my mark. Moments after accepting the invitation, I ran my hand over the spot on my left rib cage where I had my father's words tattooed a few years prior: "You are the best, you can make a difference, and you can change the world." They were my reminder every day that regardless of the scars I carried, I also carried the power to make a difference in my own life. I had the power to change my own corner of the world.

There were to be eight speakers covering a variety of different discussions about bravery. I'll admit that I questioned what I, Mallory Weggemann, a twentysomething from suburban Minnesota, was supposed to say to inspire a massive gathering of some of the most powerful and influential people on the planet, many of whom were tasked with steering their countries through political, economic, and humanitarian crises. Just the thought of it was overwhelming. What could I say that could possibly matter? Where would I even begin? And, most pressingly, *why me?*

That was when I realized the heart of my message: bravery has many faces, and the most profound acts often come in the simplest form.

"There is this mindset I had as a child," I explained from the stage on the afternoon of September 13, 2013. Looking out at the UN General Assembly—Secretary-General Ban Ki-moon sat just a few rows away from my family—I spoke as translators interpreted my words into dozens of languages:

I believed in order to make a difference and change the world you had to have a grand gesture—then I realized, we all have the ability to effect change. To be brave and fight for what we believe in, to live our daily lives with passion and heart, to rise above fear and push forward. We have the ability to smile at a passerby, free of judgment, just a simple smile to a fellow human being—acknowledging their presence. Those simple acts are courageous, they make a difference, and they change the world.

I paused and smiled, taking in the absolute insanity of this entire situation and the journey that had brought me here. I could not have imagined anything like this when my paralysis was still new. And yet, here I was, living a life of more significance, power, and opportunity than anything I dreamed of back when I could still walk.

"Live your life with passion and heart, free of fear, hate, and judgment—be courageous and know that, in any given moment, you can make a difference and you can change the world through your simple actions," I challenged the crowd.

I wheeled off the stage to a standing ovation and, afterward, shook countless hands as I met individuals from all different walks of life. It was surreal to hear policy-makers and political figures from all over the world thank me for the honesty and empowerment of my message. As I prepared to leave, a tall man with a heavy black moustache stepped forward and introduced himself as one of the senior ministry officials in Iraq. "The world needs to hear your story," he said. "We all need to hear your story." I was shaken to the core hearing those words from a man whose country was in the midst of a decade-long war and social upheaval. My dad's bedtime words were playing out more literally than any of us ever dreamed.

My visit to New York City for the UN event was made even more meaningful by the fact that Jay and I decided it was time to introduce our families to each other. In case speaking at the United Nations isn't nerve-racking enough, why not throw introducing the families into the mix, right?

My parents and sisters flew with us from Minnesota to New York, and Jay's parents, sister, and brother made their way to the city from various parts of the country. It went beautifully. Our parents connected and our siblings clearly clicked. Everything just felt right, like it was all playing out exactly as we hoped it would. Returning home to Minnesota, I found renewed confidence that with each milestone I reached and each new relationship I forged, my identity became more solidly rooted in my whole self, rather than confined to my accolades in the pool.

It may sound cliché, but as my relationship with Jay progressed, I found the best version of myself begin to surface. He helped me find the courage to confront many of the little insecurities that still plagued me since becoming paralyzed—like wearing shorts again. As insignificant as that may seem, each worry I conquered felt like another milestone toward wholeness. I wasn't living in fear or worry or questioning myself; I was simply living. Even more, I didn't see Jay as a hero for going out with a girl in a wheelchair, and neither did he. He wasn't dating me in spite of my paralysis;

he was just dating *me*, the whole person. In falling in love with Jay, I realized one more piece of my identity separate from my sport: I was a woman who was *enough*, exactly as I was.

But as life continued to open up to me, there was still one final piece of closure I deeply desired. I wanted to change the narrative of that fateful visit to the hospital that set my entire journey in motion. For years, when I shared the story of my paralysis, I usually started by saying, "On January 21, 2008, I walked into the hospital, and I simply never walked out." But that all changed in fall 2013, when, after months of physical therapy at the Mayo Clinic in Rochester, I put that unfinished chapter to rest by walking— not wheeling—out of a hospital. Even though Mayo was not the medical system where my injury occurred, I still felt empowered as—surrounded by my parents, sisters, physical therapist, and Jay—I stood five feet, nine inches tall and walked out the doors of a hospital and into a new chapter of my life.

I took each step with the assistance of a custom carbon-fiber leg braces that enabled me to stay upright and use the natural momentum and weight of my body to rotate my core and propel my legs forward. Those steps came 2,135 days late, but they came. It wasn't about the act of walking—I no longer felt the *need* to walk in order to be whole—it was about moving forward with life. While stepping out of the doors of a hospital couldn't change what happened—it could never erase the trauma I suffered—it did mean that January 21, 2008, didn't, and never will, define me.

One other significant event happened that fall: I found out that singer-songwriter Joshua Radin was coming to Minneapolis to play a concert. When Jay sent Joshua's publicist a letter to tell him that his music—and one song in particular—had helped carry me through years of recovery, Joshua replied and said he'd love to meet me. Together, we came up with an even better plan. Ahead of his concert, my family, Jay, and I all met Joshua and his band backstage; then, as he started to play the opening chords of my favorite song, I stood up and began to carefully walk with my braces, one foot at a time. They were my first steps in nearly six years outside a medical setting and without a physical therapist at my side, and each movement forward filled me with gratitude for everything and everyone that had brought me to this moment. My parents were crying, my sisters were beaming, and Jay watched me with a mix of respect and awe as I walked toward him on my own two feet. My eyes filled with tears as Joshua sang the words that were echoing in my soul: "It's a brand-new day / The sun is shining; it's a brand-new day. / For the first time in such a long, long time / I know I'll be okay."

The year following the 2012 Paralympics was one of the most significant periods of growth in my life. In rediscovering my self-worth, one piece at a time, I found myself moving even further along the journey of self-discovery. I was moving toward wholeness mentally, physically, and emotionally. When I finally recognized my value in not only what I could offer to the world but also what I inherently possessed as a person, I was no longer plagued with worries or insecurities; day by day, I found the courage to shed old behaviors and patterns of thinking. I found the joy in simply living again. When I began to understand the *why* behind my *now what?* I found the strength that already existed inside me—the power of my own flames. Everything else just became details.

Sometimes when we overcome trauma, we find ourselves on the other side, not knowing how to separate our identity from our survival. Because of the incredible effort of pushing through, we sometimes forget who we are *apart* from the fight. Our identity becomes so wrapped up in our efforts to conquer our fears or feelings of inadequacy that we lose sight of our whole self. For me, the fight was my relentless pursuit of my swimming goals. That kind of focus can propel us through the most difficult periods, but it's not enough to sustain us throughout our lives or to connect us to other people on a personal basis.

The magnitude of what we've left behind and what still lies ahead can be overwhelming sometimes, but the bravest thing we can do is to take the first small step toward our goal, and then the next, and then the next. Whether it's learning to embrace a new way of life, letting go of others' expectations for us, or confronting our personal traumas, the distance between the present and the goal can often seem insurmountable. But when we start to understand that there is meaning beyond our own struggle that connects our story to countless other people, we can begin to reach beyond ourselves. As our journey allows us to connect with and encourage others, we bridge that separation from the world that our pain has caused.

Every experience and every relationship that I developed on my own journey toward healing helped me detach my self-worth from winning. If I couldn't point to my ever-growing list of records to prove my significance, how would anyone else believe I mattered? If I no longer had medals to motivate me, what made me deserving of love? When I embraced an identity beyond my résumé and achievements, I suddenly discovered a whole other life just waiting to be lived. That didn't mean my goals as an athlete no longer mattered; it simply meant that they were part of a much bigger whole. Life was offering me so much more than just swimming. Some things were simple and satisfying, like changing my feelings about the clothes I allowed myself to wear. Some things were much bigger and more intimidating, like figuring out what to say to some of the most powerful people in the world. But instead of feeling overwhelmed by all the goals I still wanted to tackle, I realized I didn't need to conquer every dream all at once; I just needed the persistence to keep moving in the right direction.

EIGHT

REDEFINE YOUR LIMITATIONS

For me, half the thrill of living is figuring out how to challenge myself when I hear the word *can't*. When people told me I couldn't become a professional athlete or have an even better life *after* becoming a paraplegic, I set out to prove them wrong. But sometimes, even the most deeply rooted beliefs can be shaken in an instant, and that can cause us to question everything.

I believed willpower could hurtle me over any obstacle that came my way—that is, up until March 5, 2014, when the bottom dropped out of my life. Again.

———

It was still dark outside as I slid out of bed and into my wheelchair as quietly as possible. I wanted Jay—and his torn meniscus, a souvenir from our skiing trip to Colorado the previous week—to rest up as much as possible ahead of the insanely busy day we'd planned.

As I transferred myself to the shower bench and turned on the faucet, I mentally reviewed our schedule: the *Today Show*, HuffPost Live, lunch, then back to the hotel to prep for the premiere of *The Current*.

Lathering my hair, I paused for a second to enjoy the feeling of hot water against my skin—a nice break from the cold pool water that had become a staple of my morning routine. As I reached for the bottle of conditioner with my right hand, I heard a sudden crash. Before my brain could even register where the sound came from, I was on my side on the shower floor, water pouring over my mouth, my eyes, my nose, as a gaping hole in the wall revealed where the shower bench had been attached just moments before. My left arm was pinned underneath me at an unnatural angle as pain shot through my body. In a fully functional nervous system, the brain sends a message to react to a sudden shift in gravity, helping the core and leg muscles find some kind of equilibrium or a way to at least minimize the damage upon impact. As a paraplegic from the waist down, my muscles and nerves don't engage those signals from the brain in the same way. My subconscious registered the impending danger, but my body was helpless to prevent impact.

"Jay!" I tried to scream, but it came out more like a choking gurgle than a cry for help. I couldn't crawl out of the shower with only one functioning arm, and I couldn't brace myself to pull up and turn off the faucet. I opened my mouth to scream again as a blast of cold air cut through the steamy bathroom. Jay had thrown open the door, his eyes wide and panicked.

"Mal?" he shouted. "Mal, are you okay?"

I answered with equal panic. "Where are your crutches? You're going to hurt yourself more!"

Wisely, Jay ignored me. He shut off the water, wrapped me in towels, and helped me into my chair. He didn't ask for an explanation; the flattened shower bench and the hole in the wall told the whole story for me.

Shaking and crying from the fear as much as the pain, I did my best to pull myself together. I knew I needed to get to a hospital, but, foolishly, I put my fear of disappointing others ahead of my own well-being. I was in a lot of pain but decided to push through and focus on what needed to happen next for my long day of media appearances and interviews, not yet understanding how serious the injury actually was. The studio provided hair and makeup artists, so luckily I didn't need to worry about figuring out how to lift a mascara wand, let alone flatiron my hair. I looked down at my left arm, which lay limply on my lap, already swelling and turning shades of deep purple and red. *I guess that means I'm wearing the blazer I packed.*

Once we arrived on set at the *Today Show*, I left Jay to catch up with everyone while I wheeled myself into the makeup room, which was (thankfully) sequestered. I was in no shape for socializing. The woman who took care of my hair and makeup was wonderful and gave me some Tylenol. As she worked on me, I tapped into the part of my brain I usually reserved for tough workouts in the pool or weight room, reminding myself that this wasn't anything I couldn't push through. *Don't focus on what hurts,* I told myself. *Just focus on what you need to do next.*

After an admittedly great segment on the *Today Show*, Jay and

I headed to a Starbucks. It was there that I finally took off the blazer to inspect my arm, and what I saw turned my stomach. My arm was misshapen, the skin stretched and shiny over hard welts that were still forming. "Help me put my jacket back on," I snapped at Jay. I was embarrassed, frightened, and plain overwhelmed.

A few hours later, after recording at HuffPost Live, it was clear the bruises and welts were only getting worse. As I struggled to cover my arm up again, it hit me: my dress for the documentary premiere was sleeveless. I started to panic. *"What am I going to do?"* I whispered to Jay. I didn't want to show up on the red carpet with a mangled arm and pull focus away from the excitement of the event.

Luckily, I'd hired a hair and makeup artist to help me get ready for the premiere. As soon as we reached our hotel room and I showed her my arm, the wheels in her head started turning. "We'll use tattoo cover-up," she said. "It can't do anything for the swelling, but it should hide the bruises, at least." She started applying a thick, claylike material over the bruises and dusted them with powder to match my skin tone. She was exactly right—it didn't do anything to fix the distorted shape of my arm, but there wasn't a single bruise in sight. I was able to stabilize my left arm on my lap the whole night, relying on my right arm and Jay, my right-hand man, to steer my wheelchair.

The following day, we flew home to Minnesota and headed straight from the airport to an urgent care clinic. The X-rays confirmed a hairline fracture, but the doctor suspected the excessive swelling was causing additional pressure on the nerves. I prayed he was right—that the pain would subside when the swelling resolved—and left the clinic with a fiberglass brace and a modicum of hope that things would soon improve.

While I waited for my body to heal on the outside, my mental state began to deteriorate. In the weeks that followed, my fears controlled my every action. I lived in a constant state of anxiety. Terrified of falling again, I made myself a nest of pillows and blankets and slept on the floor for nearly a month. Each time I closed my eyes, my stomach dropped, imitating the sensation I felt plummeting to the floor in the hotel shower. Trials for the Pan Pac team began in three weeks in Fort Lauderdale, Florida, and—stubborn as always—I refused to drop out, even though I couldn't even get into the pool to train. My doctors advised me to lay off my practices to rest my arm, and for once, I listened, believing that I could get myself back into competition shape in no time.

My twenty-fifth birthday was just a few days before the meet, so my parents made a vacation out of it with Jay and me, spending several days with friends in Naples, Florida, before heading over to the meet. The bruises on my arm were still dark, although they now had a green tinge to them as if they were starting to heal but wanted to look as ugly as possible before they finally faded. I forced myself into the water at the local pool—my first time swimming since the fall. Gingerly, I removed the brace and bandages and carefully lowered my arm. *Maybe the cool touch of the water will be soothing*, I thought. Immediately, I realized my optimism was misplaced. Things were even worse than I'd imagined.

The moment the water touched my arm, I clapped my right hand over my mouth to keep from screaming. The pain was unbearable. My nerves felt like they were on fire, and the slightest contact sent them all into a frenzy. What was more, I realized just how much the lack of movement in my left arm restricted me; I couldn't lift it even to pull up my hair, put on my swim cap, or adjust my goggles. My arm dragged helplessly in the water when I tried to swim a lap. I had a qualifying meet in less than a week and only one functional limb. And since I was still competing as an S8, my diminished physical capabilities would be even more obvious next to the women in the other seven lanes.

In Paralympic swimming, athletes have the option of beginning their races in the water if they are unable to use the starting blocks. I had never gone that route before, as my start off the block is significantly faster. But since I couldn't even use my arms to push off the starting blocks, I had no choice. As the horn sounded to begin the 50-meter freestyle, the other swimmers dove into the pool while I took off as best I could from the water, my right arm rotating like a windmill—the only force propelling my body ahead. In London, I swam that distance in 31 seconds; that day, I touched the wall at 56 seconds—dead last—and needed a team of two people to lift me out of the water. As they hoisted me from the pool to the deck, one thought echoed clearly through my brain: *This was the dumbest idea I've ever had.* Needless to say, I didn't make the team. For me, it wasn't about trying to make the team—I went in knowing there was no chance. I showed up and raced because I had committed to it, full stop. I believe wholeheartedly in follow-through, despite how unfavorable the circumstances may be. And my circumstances were pretty unfavorable.

Back home, I sank into a deep depression. I felt more "disabled" than ever before—even more than when I first lost the use of my legs. It was as if all my hard-fought courage and independence had washed down the drain when I crashed to the shower floor. Jay had to learn how to braid my hair, how to transfer me from the bed to my wheelchair, and how to help me perform even the most basic tasks. I couldn't even steer a car by myself, so I had to rely on Jay or my parents to drive me to my twice-weekly physical therapy appointments at the Mayo Clinic in Rochester—ninety miles each way. As I watched Jay recover from his knee surgery, I was struck with a deep and irrational jealousy. His body was able to bounce back quickly from a significant injury, and he emerged good as new; my body, on the other hand, had just become more broken. With each passing day, it became clear that whatever was going on with my arm was more than merely a hairline fracture in my wrist. Regardless of how much work I put into each PT session, it felt as if I couldn't gain traction.

For the first time in my life, I couldn't simply force myself to get through it. "Mind over matter"—my guiding philosophy for every limitation I ever faced—had failed me. I didn't know how to imagine a future where my sheer force of will was not enough to push me beyond whatever obstacle lay in my path. For the first time since my paralysis, I had to actually acknowledge that I couldn't just plow my way through a challenge. I had to take a breath and accept that I was now more limited than I'd ever been before.

And it wasn't just the physical side of my game that was struggling. My fears ballooned out of control. What if I fell and couldn't get back up? What if I was alone and couldn't reach my chair? Before, I relished the challenge of figuring out a way to get myself out of a tricky situation—but that was when I had two working arms to rely on. For the first time, I felt truly trapped by my body and its limitations. It's easy, after all, to focus on our deficiencies, on what we can't do, or on what we've lost. But the slippery slope here is that our thoughts shape our feelings, which inform our actions. And our actions lead directly to our results. As my worries began to take control of my thoughts, they began to shape the way I viewed my potential. Unconsciously, I began to channel all my energy into the what-ifs rather than the hows.

I also began to question what this accident meant for my relationship with Jay. He had never known me as an athlete who wasn't at the top of her game. We didn't meet until 2011, a full three years after my paralysis; he wasn't in the picture when I had to learn how to crawl my way upstairs. He wasn't there when getting dressed by myself was cause for major celebration. He had only ever known the woman who triumphed over the challenges, who learned how to love her life when others told her she couldn't, who mowed down any obstacle that stood in her way without a second thought. He never saw me at my lowest—until now. I was terrified about what that meant for us. I wasn't worried that our love couldn't survive a dark period or that he would cut and run when the going got tough; I was scared that *I* wasn't the same person he had fallen in love with. Suddenly, I was no longer the bold, brave, audacious person who laughed in the face of whatever society told me my life as a paraplegic "should" look like. I had managed to rebuild my life completely once, but I didn't know if I had the strength to do it yet again. In fact, with each passing day, I felt more and more like a shell of the woman I used to be.

One afternoon in early June, as we pulled in to the driveway of my parents' house after another exhausting day of PT for my arm, I turned to Jay and took a deep breath. "I hate to say this," I confessed, "but I think I have to retire."

As soon as the words slipped out of my mouth, I broke down sobbing. It felt like I was breaking up with swimming, with my career, with my dreams for my life. This was the last thing I wanted; there was so much more I still felt driven to accomplish—so much more I knew I could achieve if I could just figure out a way around my present reality. I was now going to the Mayo Clinic twice a week for physical therapy and working to get to the bottom of what was going on with my arm. It felt like a continual game of hoping for the best and preparing for the worst.

Unfortunately, when I fell that day in the shower, I experienced the perfect storm between the force with which my body fell and the way I landed. We later learned that I was battling nerve damage as a result, but it would be months before I had a definitive diagnosis. It was the worst kind of déjà vu: my paralysis was challenging enough the first time, but now I felt like I was reliving it all over again with added complexities.

For me, that raw, vulnerable moment made me face the difficult question I'd been avoiding: What did I really miss about swimming—the spirit of competition or the winning itself? Did I really love the sport, or did I just love the thrill of being on top?

Jay and I developed a two-part plan to help me answer those questions. The first part came in the form of a phone call Jay placed to my old high school coach, Steve Van Dyne, about two weeks later.

"Mal needs to get back in the water," Jay explained, "and she needs a coach to help her do it. I know the two of you had a good rapport when she swam for you as a teenager. Would you consider taking her on for a couple of months while we figure this out?" Steve's answer was an unequivocal yes.

"You've got a coach," Jay said to me, a huge smile on his face as he returned home that night with my favorite comfort food, a frozen pizza. Since Jimbo moved, I felt even more lost trying to navigate this time, but it felt like a flicker of light as I fought to keep this dream alive. I prayed that Steve understood exactly what he was agreeing to take on.

Steve has always been a kind of tough-love coach, willing to kick my butt, push me, hold me back, or call me out when I needed it—and oh, how I *needed* it then. It wasn't just that I was afraid to get in the water or that I needed to relearn how to swim with adaptive strokes or the fact that I'd managed to put on twenty-five pounds during the past three months out of the water. (The frozen pizzas didn't help, either.) I needed that kind of coaching, now more than ever, because of my mental game. In a matter of weeks, I'd managed to slide from peak form to what could only be described as a hot mess, both physically and emotionally. If anyone could figure out a way to draw me out of my current situation and snap me back into the mindset of a champion, it was Steve.

School had let out for the summer, so Steve's schedule was more flexible, which meant we had plenty of time to figure out how to get me swimming again. We started each practice with simple laps in the pool: I would swim from one end to the other and then rest until I felt ready to swim back. Right away, I got frustrated—not so much with Steve, but the circumstances. "What was my time?" I'd call out when I touched the wall.

"Doesn't matter," Steve would answer.

"Just tell me," I'd beg, huffing when he shook his head again. "I want to know."

"Nope. That's not the focus right now."

Each lap was excruciatingly slow—I knew that much. I just wanted to know *how* slow so I could calculate how far off I was from my typical training times, but Steve refused to crack. He knew I would obsess over those numbers, pushing myself harder even when it wasn't safe and beating myself up when I fell short. That, of course, would cause me to continue my emotional spiral, which wouldn't do anything to help my physical performance. So exhausting lap after exhausting lap, I slogged on, coming up with creative ways to curse at Steve when I came up for air at the next wall. But this was exactly why Jay thought it was a good idea to call him in the first place. Steve knew me, and despite how frustrating the process could be, he kept me in check so I didn't let my stubbornness jeopardize my long-term goals.

The second part of our plan to help me rediscover my passion for swimming was to test out a stint as a correspondent at the Pan Pac meet in Pasadena that August. At the time, Paralympic swimming coverage was virtually nonexistent in the United States, so I offered to provide commentary, interviews, and result reports throughout the meet as someone who was part of the community and not just a curious spectator. Both companies we approached to sponsor the coverage—swim gear manufacturer FINIS and online publication SwimSwam—jumped at the offer, and we began making plans and pulling together our small but mighty team.

What followed was a week of eighteen-hour days as I covered the races, conducted interviews, live tweeted results, and edited videos to share online. I wasn't doing them alone; I had an incredible team, and among them, Jay. We loved working side by side, and this sparked our passion for production. Every day we filmed segments, talked with athletes, and reported results; and every night we worked furiously in the hotel room editing the day's stories while I wrote editorials about the importance of representation in sports. As draining as that week was, it made one thing abundantly clear to me: my love for the sport rested in the freedom that came with swimming and the community that flooded the pool decks. I loved swimming because I loved the sport itself, not because of the medals I won.

I returned to Minnesota and my training sessions with Steve with a renewed sense of purpose. I stopped panicking about my times and started focusing on how to best readapt my strokes to accommodate my injured left arm. We both knew that as my confidence returned in the pool, I would slowly but surely find my way back to myself, regaining my independence, ability to compete at an elite level, and mental edge along the way.

The day I recognized that I could no longer wait for my arm to show signs of improvement, I stopped making decisions from a place of fear and started acting instead of waiting for my circumstances to change. For months, I'd told myself that I could start training seriously once my body felt better, but I realized that I needed to seize the day and continue to take action from where

I was instead of holding out hope for a fantasy version of events that might never happen. If I waited until conditions were perfect, I might wait forever.

That change in perception made all the difference in the way I approached my first big meet since the disastrous Pan Pac trials in 2014. Rather than fixating on the body I no longer possessed, I focused on what I could do with the one I had now. I freed myself from my disappointments and allowed myself to move forward. Heading into the 2015 Para Pan American Games trials, I knew I had to be kind to myself, accepting that I now brought fears to the pool I hadn't carried before. Amazingly, I swam fast enough in my first race to earn a spot back on the national team. I was nowhere near my pre-arm-injury times, but I now had a new way to gauge myself against my competition.

The following month, I traveled to Berlin for an open meet; if I was going to race in the Para Pan Am Games in August, I wanted at least one more big race under my belt with my new body. As it turned out, I was too ambitious too soon. I swam one race and medically withdrew from the rest of the meet. But my trip to Germany was not wasted. Gazing out over the city from the roof of the American embassy after wrapping up a meeting with the ambassador, I realized my confidence and acceptance of myself had nothing to do with how many seconds I was able to drop from my previous race time and everything to do with how I responded to the opportunities that were presented to me along the way. I was much more than a Paralympic swimmer. I was a woman with a voice and a message.

With this new realization, I refocused on my speaking career when I returned home. The more I told my story onstage, the more comfortable I got speaking honestly about my human experiences rather than my accomplishments as a Paralympic swimmer. I signed a contract with a financial services organization to speak to eight different groups of executives across the West Coast—a prospect that just a year earlier would have terrified me. But now I realized my physical limitations only constrained me as much as I let them. If I looked closely, these "limitations" were actually creating new avenues for connecting, engaging, and challenging people I might never have met otherwise. People didn't care about the medals or the paralysis or the accident or any of the things that happened *to* me; they resonated with my message of resilience and the question of how we can pick ourselves up after a setback and still come back for more. The more I traveled for speaking events, the more I regained my independence. Rather than waiting until I felt like doing the things that scared me, I did them anyway. I refused to let my injury control my life any longer.

Unfortunately, this newfound audacity only lasted until June, when a recurrent infection in my arm landed me in the ER, followed by several days in the hospital hooked up to an IV drip of antibiotics. I kept my sights fixed on Pan Ams, a mere two months away, despite everything going on around me. In a follow-up appointment a few weeks after my hospitalization, I finally found the courage to ask my doctor the question that I had been too afraid to ask previously: "What is the likelihood that my arm will ever heal?"

Dr. Bengtson took a deep breath and answered, "I have suspected this for a while, but I didn't want to say anything. I think we are looking at your new normal."

My heart plummeted. The news was not a surprise, but the medical confirmation of my worst fears still sank my spirits. Yet the dire news was closely followed by a little voice in my head that whispered, *Look at what you've done* despite *the pain and immobility.* As I sat with that thought, I realized what a gift Dr. Bengtson had given me in delaying his assessment of my condition. He knew me well enough at that point to understand that swimming was more than my career—it was my lifeline to wholeness. He didn't want to see me redefine myself based on a diagnosis, so he allowed me to chase my goals before burdening me with whatever the medical textbooks said about my condition.

As I wheeled myself out of the doctor's office that day, I faced a choice. I could give in to the overwhelming urge to rush home and spend the next seventy-two hours obsessively reading every piece of literature I could get my hands on about my condition, or I could go to the pool and complete the day's scheduled training session for Pan Ams, which were in less than a month.

I'm not going to pretend that it was easy for me to drive to the pool—that I automatically put all my fears and uncertainties behind me. Not at all. But I knew I had to focus on my goals rather than my limitations. I chose to spend my energy focusing on what I was trying to accomplish rather than what I couldn't.

By the time I returned to Toronto for competition, I'd managed to shift my focus entirely. I decided to simply enjoy the experience and celebrate the fact that I was back on the international scene after more than a year away, instead of worrying about my times or rankings. I felt surprisingly relaxed as I eased into the water for my first event, the 100-meter backstroke. Contrary to every motivational speaker I'd ever heard or inspirational poster I'd ever seen, I didn't show up with winning on my mind, nor was I motivated by fear of failure.

I launched myself into the water the moment the horn sounded, pushing as hard as I could with my right arm, compensating with my core muscles. It was a good day; my left arm felt relatively loose and movable, and the topical nerve-blocking cream that dulled the pain of the water was working well. Checking the scoreboard at the end of the race, I was amazed to see that I had easily qualified for finals. A few hours later, in the medal race, I dropped another seven seconds from my time and finished third. Just like that, I was back on the podium.

I emerged from the pool absolutely beaming. I finally felt like I was starting to return to my old form and get it into gear when it mattered most. A few days later, something similar happened with the 200-meter individual medley; I raced a personal post-arm-accident best in prelims and then had another major time drop in finals, allowing me to capture gold. I swam five events in total and medaled in all of them: two golds, two silvers, and a bronze.

After each race I looked to the stands to see my team—Jay, my parents, and Steve—cheering like mad and hugging one another. Together, they had supported me, cheered for me, fought alongside me—and sometimes even fought *with* me—never doubting that I would give it my all. Even if I never won another race, we had gotten this far together, and that was a whole lot more than we were hoping for even twelve months earlier. Against all odds, I had managed to change my story yet again. Looking at the collection of medals that now hung around my neck, I had another amazing realization: we were exactly one year out from the 2016 Paralympics, and it looked like I just might have a shot at Rio, even after all I'd been through. I can't even say that the 2015 Pan Am Games exceeded expectations because I truly didn't have any expectations going in. I simply wanted to know what my body could do. Turns out, I was capable of a whole lot more than anyone realized—including myself.

This, I believe, is the heart of every person's journey. We all have an inherent desire to be recognized and celebrated for everything we can do and everything we have accomplished instead of being characterized by what others may perceive as a loss. Our ability to succeed in this pursuit lies in the truth that *we* define our limitations; our limitations don't define us unless we allow them to do so. When we are afraid of reliving a trauma, an embarrassment, or a hurt, we end up making decisions from a place of fear. We are afraid of the possibility of coming in last, so we never even try. And you know what? Sometimes we do have sad, angry, or rough days. Sometimes we *do* come in dead last. But the difference between first place and last is infinitely smaller than the difference between last place and never even having tried.

It became clear that while three of my four limbs are significantly affected due to my injuries, those restrictions were far from my biggest obstacle. I had to overcome the self-doubt and fear that threatened to keep me from the water and from all that life has to offer. After my fall in the shower, I retreated inside myself for a while, letting my trauma control me. And when I finally did take a few cautious steps forward, I wanted to erase my accident and everything that came with it by pushing myself harder than was healthy.

But life doesn't work that way. We can't give in to our limitations, but we can't ignore them either. Instead, we have to redefine them, which requires active effort on our part. We must invest ourselves into pushing beyond whatever perceived restrictions our bodies, brains, or backgrounds can put on our lives. We can't wish away our circumstances or passively hope they will change on their own. It is up to each one of us to reshape, reimagine, and redefine the limitations in our lives—every single day, with every decision we make. When we redefine our limits, we redefine what is possible.

This doesn't mean that once you redefine them, those limitations will never try to creep back in. I'd have to fight back against the fears, the anger, the depression many more times after my path changed. I'd have to learn that it is okay to experience joy following heartbreak, just as it is okay to feel the depths of pain again, no matter how much time has passed. I'd have to remind myself that healing isn't chronological; it doesn't happen on a neat, convenient timeline. It isn't a perfect process that resolves itself once and goes away forever. Loss, adversity, hardship, grief—those can be every bit as real and every bit as traumatic to the body and mind as physical injuries. Our bodies and our brains can hold on to pain that makes it difficult to move forward; yet, if we don't move forward, we run the risk of leading a hemmed-in life that reflects all the opportunities we *didn't* take and the joy we never even tried to chase.

That September, Jay and I took a much-needed vacation to Hilton Head with some friends. We had been dating for nearly three years, yet every photo we had was a selfie. Despite having gone to events together for our careers, we had chosen to keep our relationship private; therefore, we never walked the red carpets together or engaged in photo opportunities side by side. I mentioned to Jay that it might be nice to have some photos taken on the beach while we were there to have something other than a selfie to hang on our photo wall at home. He agreed and told me he would handle all the arrangements.

The ocean and the sea breeze proved to be the final piece I needed to lift me out of the depression that had plagued me since my arm injury. It was almost as if the central message of *The Current*—that water is incredibly healing for the soul—was proving itself true in my life, yet again. As we posed for the photographer, my smile was genuine. I felt hopeful and happier than I had been in over a year. As Jay and I leaned in toward each other at the photographer's request, I heard an engine rumbling in the background.

"It's 5:27," the photographer remarked, which seemed like a totally pointless comment to make, but Jay nodded.

We posed again, then Jay smiled a little and said, "Hey, Mal, look up." Confused, I looked to the sky to see a plane flying a sign that read, "Mallory, will you marry me? Love, Jay."

My mouth fell open, and when I turned back to look at him,

Jay was kneeling in the sand with an open ring box. He reached for my right hand, explaining that he had commissioned the jeweler to create a European-style ring designed to be worn on the right hand so it would not interfere with the splint I now wore on my left hand full-time. As he expressed the depths of his love and anticipation for our future, I was overcome with emotion—there in that moment I looked to a man who represented everything I wanted in this life and more. I managed to squeak out my response: "Yes, of course I will marry you!"

A few minutes later, as we walked down the beach, my parents made a surprise appearance with a bottle of champagne as fireworks began to shoot up from behind a sand dune. It was surreal—the setting, the surprise, and the fact that Jay had managed to secure all the necessary permits to pull off his crazy vision for the proposal. In that moment, as I stared up at the sky with Jay, I reflected on my life post-paralysis and my initial fears over what my future would hold. At age eighteen, I'd been uncertain if I would ever truly find joy, love, and a partner to share my life with. But life opened up the more I chose to redefine my own limitations, and I saw my greatest hopes and dreams—falling in love, getting married, and eventually starting a family of my own—materialize into my own limitless realities.

NINE

BE WILLING TO FAIL

Success doesn't come from reaching the top, it comes from something far more priceless than any tangible object or achievement could ever be. It isn't determined by gold medals, but rather defined by the journey—it comes in making the conscious choice to give your all every single day, in showing up when it is easier to back down, and in your willingness to fail just for the chance to see what you are truly capable of. Success is looking back and knowing that you did everything in your power to navigate your days with integrity, courage, humility and compassion—while simultaneously honoring your desires to be all that you dream possible.

—FROM PERSONAL JOURNAL, SEPTEMBER 21, 2016

The fall of 2015 started out like a dream. A few weeks after we returned from Hilton Head, Jay's sister Caitlin teamed up with my sisters to throw us an engagement party. Jay and I spent the weekend celebrating our engagement with family and friends, daydreaming not just of our wedding itself but of the life we were building—together.

For the first three years of our relationship, we had chosen to keep it private; our family and friends shared in our journey, but the world outside knew us only as business colleagues. We didn't do that for secrecy, but for privacy. We wanted to allow our love to grow without the pressure of expectation from society. In a world so preoccupied with social media, there was something beautiful about enjoying each milestone for what it was, instead of turning it into a social media post or a talking point in a media interview. That fall, however, we finally shared our relationship publicly. I reveled in the thrill of being newly engaged, planning our wedding, growing as a speaker, and anticipating life with my best friend. It felt like my life was moving forward again.

By the end of October, however, it became evident that my left arm was infected yet again. Within an hour of checking in to the Mayo Clinic for my appointment, my medical team had declared my condition serious enough to warrant an immediate peripherally inserted central catheter, or PICC line, to begin administering antibiotics. I have always been squeamish with needles, so the idea of having someone insert a glorified IV into the main artery of my right bicep and feeding a tube fifty centimeters through my body toward my heart made my skin crawl.

I was discharged that afternoon with a dressing on my arm to hold the cord of the PICC line in place and a folder of self-care instructions: flushing the line, administering IV infusions three times daily, and cleaning protocol before and after each step. Thankfully, since my mother is a nurse, she was able to help us make sense of it all, and a home-care nurse came from an agency every other day to follow up. Jay and I had countless alarms set as reminders for my morning, afternoon, and late-night infusions. A few days into our "new normal," we both woke up in the middle of the night to disconnect my infusion and flush my line. Fumbling through the process half-asleep, we looked at each other and laughed from pure exhuastion as we said in unison, "We are *so* not ready for kids." Those difficult weeks hardly seemed the stuff of storybook romance, and yet, there was Jay, at my side, day in and day out. It wasn't the bliss we imagined being newly engaged, but we couldn't change that; all we could do was draw reassurance from the knowledge that, regardless of what came, we were going to face it together.

Thankfully, the infection eventually cleared, and I eagerly returned to the pool, determined to make up for the training time I had lost. We were now well within the one-year mark of the 2016 Games, and each day counted if I wanted to make my second Paralympic team. As the holidays approached, everything finally started to fall into place. I began to catch my stride in training, Jay and I set our wedding date, and we began the planning in earnest. Jay's parents came to Minnesota from Connecticut for a visit after Christmas, and both our moms came dress shopping with me. On December 30—one year ahead of our wedding—we all enjoyed dinner together at the Saint Paul Hotel, our reception venue. I could see 2016 opening up before me, and it was filled with lots of love, celebration, and significance.

The following morning, I showed up for practice ready to

close out 2015 strong. A traditional New Year's Eve workout in the swimming world is 100×100s (100 rounds of either 100 meters or 100 yards each, depending on the pool), but since my body couldn't tolerate that amount, we modified it to 50×100s. It wasn't the distance I was swimming that made the workout special, though; I had my people swimming with me. Lap after lap, I looked to my left and right and saw a pool lined with my tribe, the very people who got me back into the water and guided me after my arm injury: my coach, Steve; his daughters Ashley (age fourteen), Paige (twelve), and Alexa (eight); and in the lane right next to me was Jay—faithful Jay, who is by his own admission not a swimmer. (In college he was a kicker for Syracuse. He started swimming alongside me to show moral support, and while he couldn't necessarily keep up with me, that didn't stop him from joining.) And on the pool deck, Steve's wife, Shelly, coached us all. With each stroke, I found courage and confidence—the sureness that exists when you are surrounded by people who believe in your dreams, even when you question them yourself.

Unfortunately, that self-assurance faded after the glow of the holidays. My tribe was still firmly in place and unwavering in their support, but as the Games drew nearer, the ongoing challenges with my arm injury seemed to reopen all the wounds I'd spent years healing following my paralysis. Even though I knew by that point that healing was not chronological, I still felt defeated by the fact that eight years later, I was battling to heal—again—and this time proved even harder than the first. More and more, I struggled with being alone. I panicked whenever I was by myself, whether in the house or even the place that for years felt sacred to me:

swimming over the black line. I couldn't seem to get over the fear of being alone in case something went wrong with my body, even if I was safe at home or in another familiar environment. It didn't matter that Steve was at the pool while I trained, coaching me from the deck; I felt isolated in the water. It was supposed to be the place that provided me safety and comfort, but now it just felt like a breeding ground for all my anxieties.

In the water, I felt out of control in my own body. In the shower following workouts, the lingering fear of falling hit me each time I closed my eyes to wash the shampoo out of my hair and imagined the bench tearing out of the wall again. At home, I felt trapped by a body so different from the one I had learned to love. I searched for ways to drown out those fears—music, coloring, cooking—anything to distract me from my anxieties. I clung to the belief that, with time, my anxieties would pass. Grief is funny that way; when it strikes the second time, it carries the scars that formed the first time, too—but it also reminds us that we have survived once before and we can again. With that in mind, I shifted my view from trying to "fix" myself to focusing on the comfort my tribe provided and drawing strength from Jay by my side as a beacon of hope for a better, beautiful future. Still, the emotional battle raged on.

For years, I fixed my mind on "controlling the controllable"—that is, choosing to focus on those things I *did* have the power to change as opposed to those I didn't. Challenging myself to swim again was a huge part of that mindset following my paralysis; now, because of the way my arm injury was affecting my performance in the pool, I felt like the number of things I could control had been greatly reduced. With my significantly slower times and what seemed like a constant battle with my body, swimming suddenly became a reminder of everything I couldn't do, instead of my way to prove to the world everything I could accomplish. Not only had my body changed, but my reputation as an elite athlete had transformed as well. I felt as though people who once viewed me as a fierce competitor now counted me out, or worse, considered me a has-been. Whatever acclaim I enjoyed after London was definitely gone. Of course, those closest to me didn't believe I was washed up, but it seemed like everyone who didn't have "love and support Mal" in their job description had given up on me. On one hand, I knew my doubters were wrong; on the other hand, how could I possibly prove myself when each day was a momentous struggle to keep going?

I was determined not to quit on myself, but my life seemed caught in a perpetual dance of "one step forward, two steps back." My mind had always been strong enough to push through the pain, but now, Steve made me stop swimming whenever he could see that my left arm was acting up.

"I'm fine," I insisted each time he called practice early, even though I knew he was right.

"Then why are you hiding your left arm behind your back?" he asked while I tried to hide the fact that it was tremoring. I looked away, guiltily. "That's what I thought. We are done for today."

For years, the fear of quitting had haunted me; I never wanted to be someone who gave up when the going got tough, and I certainly wasn't about to throw in the towel just because I didn't feel in top form. While I was working to understand that my body had changed, each practice we called short felt as if we were undermining what my body could do—as if we were quitting before I had a chance to hit the next breakthrough.

What I failed to understand was the difference between stopping versus quitting. Stopping is a temporary halt for the sake of protecting your well-being and your goals. Quitting is walking away from something that feels uncomfortable or inconvenient. I didn't want to go to Rio with a mindset that allowed me to give up on days when things didn't go my way. This is a challenge for all of us at times, I think. How do we find the balance between stopping—stepping back to refocus so we don't end up working against ourselves and our ultimate goals—and just plain quitting? We need to learn to embrace those moments of clarity when our body and mind tell us, "This is your best for right now," instead of fighting against them.

My performance was still unpredictable at best. On good days, I swam only a few seconds off my goals; on bad days, however, Steve might pull me from the water forty-five minutes into a two-hour workout if it became apparent that the nerves in my arm were spasming too badly. Those days frustrated me most because I wanted to keep pushing, to force my body to new heights, to not let my lack of function limit my capabilities.

"I can't get better if I'm not practicing," I complained to Steve.

He overruled my objections. "You're not helping yourself by pushing your body past the point of no return," he reminded me. But I didn't want to hear him.

Stopping felt too much like giving up, and that was the failure that scared me most. Giving up meant my potential was maxed out and my physical limitations had won. I wouldn't—couldn't—let that happen. Not yet. I reminded myself why I chose to fight for my dream of the Rio 2016 Paralympic Games rather than retire following my arm injury. I knew deep down this comeback wasn't rooted in my desire to prove my worth to anyone—I owed it to *myself* to see this dream through.

My resolution was challenged in April when I competed at the test meet in Rio de Janeiro, which gave me an opportunity to race at the aquatics center where I would be swimming if I made the 2016 US Paralympic team. *If.* Race after race, I finished at the bottom of the pack. "Forget medaling," I said to Jay and my mom, who had flown to Brazil for the event. "I won't even make the Paralympic team with these times."

"You'll get there, Mal," Jay assured me.

My mom agreed. "You've got this, sweetie. Just remember why you started in the first place."

Their confidence sounded great, but it rang hollow with me. We were less than six months out from the Games, and it felt as though I was fighting against my body rather than working with it. Every day I battled to tell myself "I've got this" while working with a body that argued to the contrary. In the locker room after one particularly frustrating race, my left arm was in a full tremor. When I tried to lift my bag, I dropped it and the contents scattered everywhere. It was all I could do to stop myself from screaming in frustration, pain, and anger. That moment was the perfect metaphor for my life: scattered, messy, and all out in the open. My failure was as apparent to everyone in the locker room as my cap, goggles, and underwear that were out for everyone around me to see. I couldn't do anything more than I was already doing to try to fight my way back to the top, just as I couldn't even pick up the belongings that now lay soaking wet on the floor. My heartbreak had less to do with my underwhelming performance and more to do with the gut-wrenching feeling that came with watching my body fall apart. All I could think about was how easy this all would have been to prevent—one screw tightened properly on that shower bench—and March 5, 2014, would have been just another day instead of one that permanently changed me all over again.

Just like that, I began to spiral down the same what-if rabbit hole I found myself battling after my paralysis, yearning for my life prior to the accident and wishing I could just go back and somehow change everything. All it took was dropping my bag and losing control of my own body in a public setting for years of healing to vanish. Suddenly an angry barrage of questions flooded my mind: *Why me? When will it stop? Will I ever catch a break?* The pity train that I fought so hard to avoid had arrived, and there was no slowing it down. It was as if my pride, along with my underwear, was out there for the world to see.

Just then, one of our team coaches noticed my predicament, reached for my scattered belongings, and helped me get everything back in my bag. In that moment, I took a breath and reminded myself of all I had survived, and I knew I would get through this too. Failing was okay as long as I had a community around to help me pick up—or to help pick *me* up. Somehow I had to come to terms with the fact that my body had changed, yet again. I needed to find a way to appreciate all it had done for me, rather than resent what it took from me.

Just before I left Rio to fly home, Jay called me with some

pretty spectacular news: Hershey's had selected three athletes for their ambassador team—gold medal Olympic wrestler Jordan Burrows, legendary American gymnast Simone Biles . . . and me. They chose to sponsor me even though the world could see that my times weren't breaking records anymore. Somehow, their support lifted my spirits more than any kind of reassurance Jay or my parents could offer; after all, my family *had* to back me up. Hershey's was a different story. An iconic, powerhouse American brand isn't going to sign an athlete out of pity. They didn't see me as a washed-up has-been who should have retired at the top of her game. They saw a fighter who kept coming back despite the disappointments; someone full of the potential and resilience the Paralympic movement represents.

Their sponsorship was the nudge I needed to wake up and recognize that my career wasn't a zero-sum game where if I failed to take gold, then I failed all around. It's too easy to slip into that kind of all-or-nothing thinking when working your way up again after a setback. It's one thing when you're just getting started and any kind of success—even if it's just getting out there and competing—feels like a victory and helps build momentum toward your growth. When you are staging a comeback, however, the pressure is different; you have your past record to compare against your present performance. Up against your previous accomplishments, your current "best" may seem lacking, insufficient, or even embarrassing. What I needed to realize was that my arm injury was a reset. I couldn't simply pick up where my training had left off; I was operating with a very different body now than I was when I "just" had a spinal cord injury. I couldn't expect the same results; I had to create new metrics to measure my progress and embrace my new normal.

Instead of thinking of my present situation as a continuation of my past career, I needed to think of it as its own thing, where as long as I gave all I had each day, I could count that as a victory. That meant that some days I practiced intensely, pushing my body as far as it could go; other days, success meant just getting myself to the pool and in the water for a few minutes before my arm gave out again; and, yes, there were days when success just looked like getting out of bed, getting dressed, and deciding that my body needed more rest. I began to measure victories not by the outcome, but by the investment: Did I give everything I had *that day* to accomplish my best? I can't say I was comfortable with that new yardstick right away, but the community that rallied around me certainly helped me find my value outside of my athletic performances, which kept me grounded in my personal goals rather than external definitions of success.

As we prepared for the final push going into trials for the Rio Paralympics in June 2016, I realized that now was my chance. If I wanted to see this comeback through, I had to be strong enough to put myself out there, which meant I had to build my confidence again. While the support of my community helped me through the unexpected detours along the way, they couldn't be behind the blocks, whispering encouragement that I was enough. I had to find that confidence for myself. We will always have naysayers—individuals who prefer to offer judgment and doubt. It isn't our job to prove them wrong or validate our worth to them. What's the phrase? "Haters gonna hate"? Something along those lines.

As for me, I wasn't seeking to prove myself to anyone anymore. Now, I was purely racing for that seven-year-old girl still inside me, who fell in love with the sport and kept coming back, despite countless setbacks, for no other reason than her love for the sport. I was racing for me and no one else. By the time I arrived in Charlotte for the Paralympic trials, I still wasn't entirely certain what I was capable of in my races, but I knew I was surrounded by my tribe, cheering me on every step of the way. Jay was there (of course), and my parents, too; my sisters and future in-laws were watching from home. Steve was pacing on the pool deck while his wife, Shelly, and their girls sat in the stands with my parents and Jay. All I had to do was look up and see them to remind myself that even if I came in dead last, they wouldn't love me any less.

The first day started off rough. My left arm was tremoring severely, but I mustered every ounce of strength I had not to spiral emotionally. I could choose to trust myself and Steve's coaching to draw out the very best I could offer that day, or I could allow the doubts to flood my mind and end up racing scared. Only one path would give me the chance to accomplish what I went to Charlotte to do. So I did what I knew how to do best: I put my head down and threw every ounce of strength I had at my goal. Race after race, I shocked myself with my performance; it was one of the best competitions of my career. I didn't break a single record, but that didn't matter anymore; my metric for success had changed. I knew that I gave everything I had—not just in Charlotte but in every moment that came before—and regardless of whether or not I was named to the team, my body gave me everything it could.

The day after competition ended, all the Paralympic hopefuls assembled in a large conference room while the head coach for Team USA read down an alphabetical list of names of those who had made the team. The lucky ones made their way to the front of the room, where they were given a Team USA teddy bear and a team shirt before exiting out the side door; the athletes who did not make the team exited out the door in the back of the room. Outside, family and friends stood around as they waited. Unfortunately, as a Weggemann, it was a long wait to reach the end of the alphabet, but my tribe hung tight and kept an eye on both sets of doors.

I'll never forget the looks of complete joy on everyone's face when I finally peeked around the door, shirt on and teddy bear in my lap. Not only had I made the team, but I had qualified for all seven individual events; I was still swimming as an S8 despite my additional injury that now left me with only one fully functioning limb. After a lot of hugs and plenty of tears, I couldn't help but think that even if the outcome that day had been different, this same group of amazing people would still be hugging and crying with me.

And my team wasn't done growing. In the two months between trials and the Games, a few more sponsors signed on as well, even though they knew I was still something of an underdog—but definitely a fierce one. There is just something more inspiring about fighting to the finish than sailing easily to gold, and I think my sponsors recognized that; the persistent pursuit of excellence is infinitely more valuable than any kind of flash-in-the-pan success. Winning is something that happens in a moment, but grit is about the long haul. Resilience is not something you can hold—but when you have it, nothing can hold you back.

The two weeks at the Rio Paralympics held some of the biggest triumphs and greatest heartbreaks of my career, and I persisted through them all, giving everything I could in every single stroke. During my first event in Rio, the 400-meter freestyle, my arm went numb 150 meters into the race. By the time I finally touched the wall, my arm had turned blue and my skin was cold due to lack of circulation. I didn't make finals, and instead I spent the next several hours with our sports medicine team, stretching and massaging my arm to get the blood flowing properly again, to stop the tremors, and to prepare me for the six events I still had ahead.

But that wasn't the most difficult moment of the Games for me. After days of battling with my body to hold on through each race, I reached the 50-meter freestyle—*my* race, since I was the reigning gold medalist from London and the Paralympic record holder. The horn sounded, I dove into the water . . . and thirty-three seconds later, I touched the wall. Within moments, the results appeared on the board showing the rankings from the previous heats to reveal who had made the top eight advancing to finals. There it was, on display for the world: "M. Weggemann" in eleventh place. In half a minute, I had gone from the Paralympic record holder to not even qualifying for finals. What your heart wants and what your body can provide don't always align.

In that moment, all I wanted was my people. I gathered my belongings and made my way upstairs to the stands. I wheeled over to the barricade separating the athlete zone and the spectator section where they were all waiting, and I broke down in their arms.

Their presence gave me all the comfort I needed. Yes, I was disappointed in the outcome of the race, but I was not disappointed in myself—nor was I worried that they were disappointed in me. I knew and they knew what it took to get me there and how I had fought for every lap, stroke, and breath in that pool. I also knew I was not through fighting.

I had one final event, the 200-meter individual medley, on September 17, which also happened to be my dad's birthday. I wanted nothing more than to reach the podium that night. As they announced my name, I wheeled out behind the block of lane two and looked into the stands to see my tribe front and center. It looked like they went to Party City on July 5 and bought out the entire Fourth of July clearance section. They were lined up nine strong, and the power that filled me in those final moments before my race reminded me that while I may physically hover the black line alone, I had them with me every inch of my race. I left my entire being in the pool that night, but as I came up after my finish, I didn't see a light on my starting block signifying I had made the podium. Instead, there was a 5 next to my name—fifth place. I looked to the stands and saw my family cheering wildly and my coach standing in the aisle in the stands with both hands in the air and tears in his eyes. That moment could never be defined by a medal, because there is no medal that could make it any better than it already was. It didn't matter that I slipped out of bronze medal position in the final ten meters of the race; I realized how far I'd come, turning a moment of loss into a complete victory. Despite every reason to quit, I chose to fight. Critics may count that as a failure, but if so, it was a pretty beautiful one.

While I didn't reach the podium in Rio, I never questioned my right to be there. Rio wasn't about the medals; it was about accepting disappointment with grace and the courage to come back for more. Most of all, Rio was about realizing that success is about the effort, not the outcome. Early in my career, when I swept my events or broke a record, I immediately started critiquing what I could do better to shave off a few more seconds next time. After the 2016 Rio Paralympics, however, for the first time ever in my career, I left knowing that there was not one single thing I could have done differently to have had a better outcome.

Our willingness to fail is, in fact, what leads us to our greatest achievements. When we fear failure above all else and aren't willing to take the risk, we simply never start in the first place. Every new opportunity brings with it an element of the unknown, which means a chance—maybe even a likelihood—of failure.

The Rio Games took more fight to get to and get through than any other meet of my career. They were filled with more hardship than I would have liked, but also more love than I could have ever hoped for. The contrast between my life after London and my life after Rio surprised me. Despite what may have appeared to be a far less successful Games for me, I was happier, more content, and more at peace with the life I had created now than I was four years earlier when I won my gold and bronze medals. Even though my body was less reliable than it was then, I appreciated it in a different way because of everything it had endured. I realized more than ever that it was the very vehicle that carried me toward my dreams. While I didn't reach the podium in Rio, I actually accomplished more than I could have hoped; I refused to give up on myself just because the road was difficult and I faced failure along the way.

The difference between failing and being a failure is immeasurable. Failing is simply not realizing your goals. We can't lose our focus when that happens—and it will happen. That's just life. Being a failure, on the other hand, is not meeting your potential. It's not leaning into the fullness of who you have the power to be. It's not realizing goals because you never even attempted to reach them. Failing and being a failure are *not* the same thing, though for a long time, I couldn't distinguish between the two. Not until I had a strong sense of who I was outside of the pool, an understanding of my own value and worth that wasn't rooted in winning, did I recognize the difference. Being a failure meant making my defeat part of my identity; failing, on the other hand, is just a temporary bump in the journey that helps us learn and gives us the strength to return to the fight even stronger next time.

My willingness to fail in Rio opened my eyes to the beauty of success that isn't dependent on winning. *Of course* I would have liked to have come home with a medal around my neck, but at least I'm not carrying regret on my shoulders. I can see now that the practices where I reluctantly stopped made me stronger, not weaker. I didn't quit; I simply forced myself to become okay with a new definition of success.

I returned to the States empty-handed but not defeated. In so many ways, Rio represented the greatest success of my career. I no longer equated triumph with coming in first, and I didn't beat myself up over what I should have done differently. When we learn to celebrate the intangibles—the symbolic victories that stem from who we are instead of simply what we can do—we elevate persistence, discipline, tenacity, and grit. We become better people rather than just a name in a record book. Not every victory can be quantified. When we separate success from a specific outcome, we gain a new metric by which to evaluate our lives and find the meaning that comes in the journey.

TEN

LOVE PERSEVERES

Over the years I have learned the power love possesses to weather even the greatest of storms. I have found that unwavering love knows no limits—it transcends all, bringing light to even the darkest of seasons.

—FROM PERSONAL JOURNAL, JANUARY 30, 2017

"Are you ready, Mally?" my dad asked as he hooked his right arm around my left.

I took a deep breath and nodded. I knew as we linked arms that I was about to share one of the most important walks of my life—with my dad as he led me down the aisle. As we waited at the threshold of the church, I could feel both of us relive the memories of our many walks, from our hiking trips when I was little all the way to that fateful day in January 2008 when he walked alongside me into the procedure room—the last true walk we'd taken together.

My physical therapist took the arm crutch I was using for balance, repositioned my veil, and stepped aside as the wedding coordinator fluffed the train of my dress and the string quartet began to play. The wooden doors opened into the sanctuary, and I could hear the sound of everyone standing as the opening notes of Pachelbel's Canon in D floated toward us. "Just take a deep breath," I told myself as my emotions surged. I glanced up and caught Jay's eye as he stood seventy-five feet in front of me at the altar, grinning and wiping his eyes. "Left," I whispered to my dad as I began to count our steps. And cautiously, arm in arm, we began to walk toward the front of the church.

That's right. I *walked* down the aisle on my dad's arm. Since I returned home from Rio three months earlier, nearly everything in my life was focused on preparation for this moment. My homecoming in 2016 was vastly different compared to after the London 2012 Games; I wasn't searching for my *now what?* This time, I was planning my future and celebrating the love that filled my life.

One of the best things about our wedding-planning process was that Jay was a part of every step—from meetings with our wedding planner, to finalizing our floral arrangements, to dancing around the kitchen with me as we decided on the music for our ceremony and reception. We didn't want to get distracted by focusing on the wrong things. We weren't planning for the perfect *day*; we were planning for something so much bigger: our union as husband

and wife. As nice as those little details were, we had bigger things to think about—like, just getting me down the aisle.

We weren't worried about a runaway-bride scenario; quite the opposite, in fact. The truth was, I had dreamed of walking down the aisle with my father for as long as I could remember. Thanks to the custom leg braces I had gotten made years prior, I knew I could take a few steps over a short distance, but I had not used them at all since my arm injury in 2014. Now, however, I was determined to master those braces again and live out that dream exactly as I'd always imagined it.

For two months, Jay and I made the ninety-minute drive twice a week to Rochester to work with my physical therapy team at the Mayo Clinic; my parents came along when they could as well, so Dad and I could practice. The challenge, of course, wasn't only that I couldn't move or feel my legs; in my floor-length wedding dress, I wouldn't be able to see them either, which made concentrating on balance while my feet swung forward outside of my control even more daunting. First, I practiced in front of tall mirrors to get used to the sensation of moving while standing at my full height again. After several weeks, I advanced to wearing a full-length petticoat to imitate my gown.

Of course, in true Mal fashion, I didn't *just* dream of walking; I wanted to walk arm in arm with my father. I wanted to stand throughout the ceremony and walk with Jay down the aisle after we were pronounced husband and wife. I wanted to stand for our first dance and the father-daughter dance. I am nothing if not ambitious.

Each session, my therapist harnessed me into the zero-gravity machine that off-loaded my weight, since my arms and core had to support and stabilize my entire body while facilitating the movement for my legs. If it sounds ridiculously complicated, that's because it was.

"Dad, don't forget. Shoulders back!" I reminded him, so we could jointly maintain our posture while arm in arm.

"I'm trying, honey," he said as he sweated. "This is a lot of pressure."

"What?" I joked. "You don't want to drop your paralyzed daughter?"

Jay, on the other side of the room, laughed while also looking nervous, knowing his turn was next. Mom sat on the side, relieved that her mother-of-the-bride duties didn't involve anything but moral support.

Through each stage of the final wedding preparations, I was reminded that the simple act of walking down the aisle was anything but simple because it carried so much symbolic and emotional weight. Not very long ago, I questioned if I would ever be able to love *myself* enough to love another person. It takes both confidence and courage to find your own worth when the world sees you as needing to be fixed or somehow "less than" just because of your circumstances. My love with Jay taught me one incredibly important lesson: love doesn't make exceptions; it is all-encompassing. Jay loved all of me, including my wheelchair.

My practice sessions at Mayo were daunting and left me sorer than some of my hardest training sessions leading to Rio ever did, because I was using muscles and postures that I hadn't really used in eight years. But there was Jay, right beside me, cheering me on at each therapy session. On our wedding day, it didn't matter to him how I moved down the aisle, as long as I met him at the altar. I didn't have to walk to be whole; I was already whole. Jay was marrying me—just *me*, exactly as I am. That's the thing about love—it doesn't seek to change you, and it isn't predicated on what you can bring to the table. Unconditional love is . . . well, unconditional. Our love isn't perfect—no love is—but that's part of the beauty. We fumble, fall, heal, and grow together; love becomes what it needs to be in the moment or the season, evolving and adapting, but never wavering.

As I looked at my reflection in the mirror for my final dress fitting, I caught my breath. The confidence, strength, and peace I longed for seemed to radiate from my soul. This wasn't superficial or fleeting happiness; this was deep-seated joy. I found myself feeling the one thing I never knew if I would feel: bridal. It wasn't because I was standing at five feet, nine inches tall rather than sitting, and it wasn't because I had the perfect dress (although it was a dream). It was simply because the reflection looking back at me was one of a woman who had found herself on the other side of loss. Her worth, being, and love weren't encompassed in tangibles; they were rooted in the freedom that comes with knowing her own worth. My walking wasn't about the need to leave my wheelchair in order to feel beautiful; it was about my desire to control my own destiny and write my own story.

Unfortunately, my arm continued to deteriorate throughout that autumn, which threatened to throw a wrench into all my wedding goals. I was a grown woman and two-time Paralympian, but I couldn't even pick out limes in the produce section without dropping them because my arm would seize up. Despite what

I told myself, everything was *not* okay. In November, Jay and I made the difficult decision to cancel our honeymoon as it had become clear my arm was getting worse by the day. Still, we had the wedding itself to look forward to, and all the meticulous planning we'd put into it. A wedding is not just about the event, after all; it's about marking the moment when two lives, two families, and two circles are forever blended. For Jay and me, the process of planning our wedding was as much about introducing our two worlds—his friends and family from the East Coast and mine from the Midwest—as it was about exchanging our vows. We couldn't wait to celebrate both the love and support of our communities, as well as the love we had found in each other.

And so, on December 30, 2016, I linked my father's arm with mine and carefully placed one foot in front of the other. It took me close to five minutes to make my way down the aisle. We passed loved ones who hadn't seen me walk since I was paralyzed and others who had only known me in a wheelchair. Just before we reached the altar, we paused long enough for me to hug my mom— for one last moment with my parents, just the three of us—and I felt the depths of pain we had faced together fill with love. Here we were, living proof that good overcomes. Then my father and I took our final steps, and Jay assisted us as we climbed the steps of the altar. I let go of my dad's hand, gave him a kiss on the cheek, and turned to Jay. After years of navigating through my greatest heartbreak following my paralysis, I found that in the end it led me to my deepest love.

The significance of everything about our ceremony was beautifully profound—not just that I stood for the entire ceremony, but the symbolic rituals we incorporated too. We felt the power of love surround us as we looked out to the congregation and guests came forward to take communion. We celebrated the metaphor of blending our roots, mixing soil from my childhood home in Minnesota and his in Connecticut to one day plant a tree for our children. This all led us to the moment when we stood, eye to eye, as we vowed to love, respect, and honor one another before our family, friends, and God. Moments later, our pastor spoke those consecrating words: "For those whom God has joined, let no one separate." Then Jay and I shared a kiss and walked, together, into our future.

At the reception, I had my first dance with Jay and then one with my father before changing into my "sitting" dress and taking my leg braces off. The walking portion of our wedding day was everything I dreamed it to be, but I also didn't want to pretend as if my wheelchair wasn't a part of who I am; I felt every bit as radiant seated on four wheels as I did standing on my own two feet. (Not to mention, Jay and I can rock a wedding dance floor.) We danced the night away celebrating the incredible life we were about to embark on, together, surrounded by love.

To make up for our canceled honeymoon, my sisters treated Jay and me to a night at a boutique hotel in Minneapolis about two weeks later. But, in true Minnesota fashion, we were socked with sub-zero temperatures and blowing snow. Instead of the fancy dinner out we had planned, Jay and I holed up in our hotel room with pizza and a bottle of wine while we got lost in dreams of what our future would hold. It wasn't a tropical beach, but it didn't have to be. I was with my man, and that was all that mattered. After all, life isn't about searching for the perfect moment, but rather finding joy amid the imperfections.

And, let me tell you, there were *plenty* of imperfections in those first months of marriage. My left arm continued to worsen, and I could barely move it to wheel my chair, let alone to swim. By the end of January, we were knee-deep in medical appointments, whether it was physical therapy twice a week at the Mayo Square in Minneapolis or making the long drive to Rochester for tests and procedures at the Mayo Clinic. As quickly as I had found my new normal following my paralysis nine years earlier, I could see that would not be the case with my arm injury. I was now two years post-accident, and my body was still struggling to adapt. The independence that had proved so essential to my healing last time eluded me now; I needed more help than Jay alone was able to provide. Rather than moving out of my parents' house following the wedding, it became clear we needed the extra set of helping hands as we tried to find our new normal. It wasn't a typical newlywed arrangement, but then again, nothing about our lives was.

We joked that living with my parents was like having a pair of fun roommates. We took turns making dinner and arranged March Madness bracket tournaments for the house. My parents' yellow Lab, Sam, also got into the fun, and he not only exploited all four of us for belly rubs but also slowly began transferring his loyalty over to Jay and me. During the day, when everyone else was at work or out of the house, Sam would nose his way into our room and curl up on the bed with me so I could alternate between loving on him and crying on him. Sam was as worried about me as the rest of the family was, because, behind the laughter and jokes, I sank into a deep depression.

Nothing made sense to me. Never before had I felt simultaneously more surrounded by love and more adrift. Everything became infinitely easier to bear with Jay by my side, but it also seemed so much harder because it wasn't what I thought life after marriage would look like. My medical team pulled me from the pool until we could figure out what was going on with my arm, and without the water, I felt lost. Swimming wasn't just my career, it was also my therapy—where I worked through the depths of loss, heartbreak, and struggle. Now, as my body betrayed me, I no longer had my sanctuary in which to work through my feelings. Each day that I struggled with simple tasks, I feared Jay would feel like there had been a bait and switch, wherein the strong, confident, happy woman he married became a broken, helpless one almost overnight. The "in sickness and in health" aspect of our vows became our reality immediately following our wedding, but in truth, it had always been a part of our relationship.

Thankfully, Jay took everything with his usual optimism and humor. In the evenings, as we sat in our room above the garage at my parents' house, he found ways to make me laugh by reminiscing about some of the crazy stories that seemed perfectly normal to us.

"Remember our first medical appointment together?" he asked.

"When the container overflowed, leaving a puddle of my pee at your feet." I laughed. "How could I forget?"

"Followed by lunch at Jimmy John's. That had to have been our most romantic date yet," he said.

Yes, my husband came to a urine study with me when we were dating. Yes, sometimes things like that are part of my normal as an individual living with a spinal cord injury. And yes, I basically peed at his feet. Yet here we were, three years down the road, married, despite the puddle on the floor that day. Now my biggest concern wasn't my bladder capacity, but battling through an injury that threatened to derail everything I'd worked to build. But we knew if we held on to each other and a sense of humor, we could face anything. Sure, there would be days I might feel down—maybe even entire seasons—but now that we were married, it wasn't my job to remain strong at all times, just as it wasn't his. We quickly learned that as long as one of us could remain strong enough to carry both of us through, we would be okay, because our life was a team sport now.

In April, I was inducted into the Minnesota Swimming Hall of Fame alongside Olympic swimmer David Plummer. The annual ceremony takes place in conjunction with the All-State Banquet, which is held for the top eight high school swimmers in each event. My family, Steve, Jay, and I attended to celebrate an honor I never even entertained as a possibility when I was younger. During the induction, I leaned over to Steve, who remembered my mediocre high school swimming career as well as I did, and joked, "Who would have thought that a swimmer who never even made it to state, let alone the honors banquet, would be getting inducted into the hall of fame?" Amazingly, Steve did not have a snappy comeback for me in the moment; instead, his pride trumped his sense of humor.

That night, I felt my swimming career come full circle as Steve introduced me to the attendees. Sitting onstage, I looked around at a room that represented the Minnesota swimming community—one I had been a part of for as long as I could remember, and more than that, one that welcomed me with open arms when I needed it most. I felt the love of every person who had shaped my athletic journey; not just the inner circle of my family, but my old teammates, my coaches, the officials, and all the parents and fans who had cheered in the stands for their swimmers since my first race at age seven. My love for the sport was just as strong as it had ever been, and while I was facing undesirable circumstances, that love continued to drive me forward. It was the reason I had reentered the water in the first place, and the reason I couldn't bring myself to hang up my suit just yet. The road was so long and the way still so unclear that only a true love for swimming could have kept me moving—and that's exactly what happened.

That May brought another round of tests and procedures at the Mayo Clinic, and after being poked and prodded at more doctors' appointments than seemed possible, I had some difficult decisions to make with very real implications for the future of my career. Thankfully, the thoracic surgeon managing my case was not just one of the best in his field, but also tremendously compassionate. He took great care as he guided us through the decision-making process. Surgery was no small undertaking; my chest would have to be opened from my collarbone to my rib cage so that the doctor could remove the scar tissue on my brachial plexus (the nerve bundle that runs from the spine to the end of the arm). He also would have to remove two muscles from my neck and my top rib on the left side in order to salvage what he could of the nerve. The delicate procedure itself would last six or seven hours. He would have to time each cut with the expansion and contraction of my lungs. In fact, I was warned ahead of time that I might come out of the surgery requiring a chest tube, since the chances of puncturing the lung were fairly high. To say I was utterly terrified would be an understatement, but I knew it was the best decision not only for my career but also for my quality of life.

Thankfully, my entire medical team went the extra mile to prepare me. We already knew I would likely have a hard time going into or coming out of anesthesia due to the flashbacks I often faced in medical settings, so the staff permitted my parents and Jay to stay with me right up until I was rolled into the operating room. When I squeezed my husband's hand as the nurses rolled my bed down the hall toward the OR on the morning of June 21, 2017, I felt centered and supported. The surgery went off without a hitch; there were no issues on the physical side and no flashbacks on the emotional side.

Afterward, however, was a different story. My recovery was brutal, and the emotional toll even worse as I struggled with feeling more helpless than ever before. I was never alone, though. Jay slept on a cot in my room every single night for the two weeks I spent in the hospital. He only ever left my side to take a shower or to grab a short nap in the hotel room where my mom was staying. When Jay left, my mother was right there to take his place. Still, I struggled. How could we possibly be back here yet again? The trauma to my body from the surgery was so intense that I needed a team to lift me just to get me out of bed since my upper body couldn't bear the weight of me transferring myself. Even when my care team managed to move me from the bed to the recliner in my room, I couldn't sit upright for more than a few minutes or my blood pressure would skyrocket. Each day felt like I was moving backward rather than forward, but the people around me filled my room with love.

On June 30, Jay and I celebrated our six-month anniversary. He brought roses and take-out pizza, and we sat in my hospital bed and had a picnic. Even in the darkest moments, there are ways to celebrate; you simply have to make the choice to do so. Instead of dwelling on everything that moment was not, we made the choice to honor it for what it was, and to make the most of it exactly as we could. Rather than waiting for conditions to be "right" to be joyful, we found what joy we could in the moment.

When I was finally able to go home, I struggled with even the most basic tasks, like lifting my arms to brush my teeth or dressing myself. Pushing my own wheelchair was out of the question. For years I had insisted that I would *never* use a power chair; now, I was completely immobile without one. My independence, which had been the cornerstone of my identity for so long, was gone. So was swimming, my favorite way to process life and let my mind work through whatever it needed to resolve. The things I loved—the things that made me who I am—were off-limits.

For weeks following surgery, I couldn't travel, which meant that my speaking career—something that had surprisingly become as much a part of my professional identity as swimming—was virtually nonexistent. Thankfully, one of my corporate clients graciously offered to broadcast my speech virtually to their conference attendees rather than just canceling. When the event rolled around, I did my hair and put on makeup for the first time in nearly two months. It didn't matter that it took me almost three times longer than usual to get ready; I briefly felt a glimmer of myself surface.

"I don't feel like myself," I cried to Jay afterward. "People look to my speeches for empowerment and motivation. My job is to connect with a room full of strangers and help them feel empowered to effect positive change in their lives, even if it's just getting themselves out of bed in the morning. But I can't even do that myself!"

"Mal, I know it's tough," Jay reasoned. "But remember what we always say. Even if we can inspire and empower just one person, it's worth it."

I realized he was right. While I was struggling, remembering my *why* gave me the strength to push forward through another day. That's the great thing about love. It reflects your best self back to you.

While I battled to find my way back, there was one place I could go that felt like an escape. If I couldn't physically dive into the pool, I decided, I could at least visualize myself there. I would close my eyes and imagine the sensation of the water as it moved through my hands, the sound as it washed over my ears, and the beauty of the black line below me guiding me forward. To my surprise, the practice worked. Even though I wasn't anywhere close to returning to the pool, I felt myself start to stir back to life. Slowly, I forced myself to try little things that might help me find my way out of the darkness. I planted a small herb garden just to give me something to tend. I taught myself to knit in an effort to prevent losing what few fine motor skills remained in my left hand. It was slow going, but at least I was accomplishing something. I even began cooking again once I was able to pull a cutting board and some vegetables onto my lap. I certainly wasn't making five-star meals, but at least I had the satisfaction of creating something. Facing the uncertainty of my body felt all-consuming, but I never stopped fighting. Despite how challenging it was, deep down I knew this, too, would pass. Yes, it was difficult, but I knew that it could be worse, and I had a choice in how I responded—so I chose to rally.

By the end of the summer, I gradually began to travel again with Jay for speaking events. While I enjoyed getting back to something like my old routine, I struggled with how much I had changed. I no longer had feeling through my neck and chest; my breathing on my left side was affected, so talking for more than a few minutes at a time left me gasping for air; and a massive scar now stretched across the left side of my chest. I had to relearn how to love my body once again.

Meanwhile, I was still attending physical therapy sessions twice a week in an effort to restore movement to my left arm. As my incision healed, my range of motion improved, but the violent

tremors continued. It became clear that I might need a second surgery to decompress the nerves further. The idea of doing it all over
again was deflating. I wasn't swimming, I couldn't drive, and I had
barely begun to start wheeling myself again. Yes, my visualization
exercises helped me get back to some kind of a normal life, but I
was emotionally exhausted and worn down by the effort it took
simply to get through the day, let alone to pick myself up again
after every repeated setback. Every little gain I made seemed to
instantly be undone by something else. I couldn't catch my breath,
and I couldn't catch a break.

Then, in October, Jay had a work trip to Athens, Greece, and it
struck me as the perfect opportunity to steal a little time with my
sister Jessica. She was going through a divorce and I was battling
depression, so I figured we could both use a short escape from
our present realities. I had flight benefits from all my travels, so
I booked us an impromptu long weekend in Greece—the kind of
crazy, unplanned escape that can help pull you out of a rut.

Over our four days there, Jessica and I wandered through the
streets of Athens while Jay worked, and we even took a day trip to
some of the nearby islands. We were both facing so much change
in our lives, but for a few days we were able to disconnect from
reality and find solitude just talking and sharing an adventure
together. We cried about the pain of broken dreams. We laughed
about childhood memories. (*I* laughed about a bird pooping on
Jessica as we were sharing a bottle of wine in an outdoor café in
the sun.) The spontaneity of the trip offered a reminder that there
is beauty in the world, even when your own corner of it is dreary.
Sometimes, stepping away from the stress and pain to simply *be*

with someone who knows you better than just about anyone else— and loves you anyway—can give you the strength to keep fighting.

And just then, strength was exactly the thing I needed. Less than two months after our trip, I went back to the Mayo Clinic for another surgery, this time to detach my pectoral minor muscle due to its continued compression of the brachial plexus nerve.

My recovery from that second surgery in December was shorter, thankfully, but that was due in part to another unexpected break from my everyday life and a remarkable young woman I met three weeks later in Atlanta. Grace was a fourteen-year-old survivor of osteosarcoma, a pediatric cancer that had resulted in the partial amputation of one of her legs. Many people might have counted that amputation as a loss, but not Grace. Instead, it fueled her new dream of becoming a Paralympic swimmer. Unfortunately, though, her cancer had returned—and this time there was little her doctors could do for her. Grace's family attended the same church as one of Delta's executives, and since I served as a member of the advisory board on disability for the airline, my colleagues reached out to see if I would be willing to fly down to Atlanta and meet with her. The plan, they explained, was a lunch with the executive team and then a tour of the training facility where Grace and I might be able to swim together in the pool that crews use to practice for water evacuations. I was thrilled to meet with Grace, but I was only three weeks out of my second surgery and had not been in the water for over a year. I knew this visit was much larger than swimming, so I packed my suit and figured I'd make the call about the pool when I got there.

Grace and I spent a fantastic afternoon together and discovered that we shared the same birthday, something that deep down felt as if it represented divine intervention—not fate, not even serendipity, but rather, intention—as if our worlds were meant to collide. Then, as we were headed for the pool, Grace looked at me and asked, "Are you going to swim with me?"

One glance at her eager, beaming smile and every bit of caution went out the window. Without thought or hesitation, I got in the water with Grace. Here was a young girl facing odds no child should know, and she was doing so with bravery, humor, and (fittingly) a tremendous amount of grace. I knew in that moment that swimming with Grace was absolutely the right thing to do, and it was one of the greatest gifts I have ever received. We were fighting different battles, but we were both driven by a love and a passion that filled our hearts with courage. As we enjoyed our shared love of the water, I felt the power of love, hope, and so much faith. Even though Grace's diagnosis was dire, she didn't give up; her faith guided her forward, giving her the courage to know that her journey was about something so much larger than herself. "Courage is not eliminating fear," Grace told me. "Courage is not letting fear eliminate hope."

After that visit, both Jay and I felt a calling to do more. Grace had found the courage she spoke of, not only to live her life to the fullest, but also to use her voice to champion change. She chose to share her story in an effort to raise awareness so children in the future could have more options for treatment or even a cure. It was as if my dad's words rang true for Grace as well: "You are the best, you can make a difference, and you can change the world." We wanted to help her in her mission, so we reached out to a good friend and colleague who is the president of NowThis, a social media news company. After connecting with Delta and coming up with a plan for maximum impact, we all joined forces to put together a short documentary about Grace, which we shot during her final weeks in hospice care. Interviewing her teachers, swim coach, and friends, we watched as her community raised umbrellas, a symbol of faith that Grace inspired: it isn't enough just to hope for the rain; we must carry our umbrellas and believe that the rain is really coming. She passed away on March 25, 2018, one day before her fifteenth birthday, but the love she stirred in so many people lives on.

Reflecting on her story, I was amazed to realize that though I only spent one day with Grace, the impact she had on me—and everyone around her—was profound. Her story touched countless lives because of the ripple effect of her courage and faith. Grace's buoyancy and strength even inspired Ed Bastian, the CEO of Delta, to commit to running the New York Marathon that fall and to raising $1 million for pediatric cancer research (a goal he almost doubled). Watching the outpouring of love she inspired made me take a step back to recognize the same sort of love that surrounded me—and had been surrounding me—all my life. As I thought about the capacity of love to support, encourage, empower, and carry us, I realized that love was the key to lift me out of the darkness that had settled over me for so long. Just as we have a choice as to how we will react to our circumstances, we also have a choice as to which way we will allow the water to take us when it closes over us. Will we sink or will we rise? Grace chose to rise. Her cancer wasn't stronger than the love and faith that enveloped her, and my injury and depression were not stronger than the love and faith in my own life. Too often, we think of "buoyant" people as light, cheery, and maybe even a little carefree, but the truth is, buoyancy is not for the faint of heart. It requires toughness, resilience, and a lot of personal grit. Buoyancy isn't about sunniness; it's about persistence.

Two weeks after I met Grace in Atlanta, I celebrated the tenth anniversary of my paralysis—a tradition I now called my "Cheers to Wheels." I have found the beauty that lies in what happened in January 2008 and the journey on which it has taken me. It gave me the gift of perspective, allowing me to feel the depths of love, to appreciate the simplicities in life, and, above all, to know the difference between simply being alive and truly living. That spring, which began with marking a decade in my wheelchair and ended with a celebration of Grace's life, I realized that despite all the recent setbacks and disappointments with my arm, I was surrounded by love. I hadn't just survived the previous decade; I found the beauty that lies on the other side of loss. I built a life that had sustained the depths of heartbreak and nurtured a love so pure that it persevered through even the greatest odds.

No matter how much time passes in my life, I can feel the rawness of the heartbreak I experienced in the days, weeks, and months following my paralysis—questioning whether I would ever be worthy of love, uncertain if it would ever get easier to see my own reflection. It was as if I were drowning in my fear of the unknown. And yet here I was with a life still marked by pain, but also filled with an unimaginable amount of love. Life is not an "either-or"—love *or* pain. It is always both. In order to know the true heights of love, we have to crawl through the depths of pain; the only thing that pulls us through those depths is love. We have to force ourselves forward, guided by love, before we can fully appreciate the scope of what we have endured.

I have created a life anchored in love. Everywhere I look, I find myself reminded of that fact. I have the love of my husband. The love of my family. The love of a community. The love of my own self as I celebrate my own inherent worth as a human being. Nothing lasts forever—not circumstances, not darkness, not even life. Nothing except love. Love is sleeping on a cot in a hospital room for weeks at a time. Love is snapping into action when someone or something inspires you to reach beyond yourself. Love is a community rallying around you. In the midst of my darkest period, I didn't have swimming to get me through—I had love.

In our wedding ceremony, we included the famous "love passage" from 1 Corinthians 13:4–8, 13:

> Love is patient, love is kind. It does not envy, it does not boast, it is not proud. It does not dishonor others, it is not self-seeking, it is not easily angered, it keeps no record of wrongs. Love does not delight in evil but rejoices with the truth. It always protects, always trusts, always hopes, always perseveres.
>
> Love never fails. But where there are prophecies, they will cease; where there are tongues, they will be stilled; where there is knowledge, it will pass away. . . . And now these three remain: faith, hope and love. But the greatest of these is love.

Our wedding day served as a reminder that love is more than just a feeling; it is an action driven by the choices we make. In his toast at our wedding, my father shared the quote Maya Angelou made famous: "Love recognizes no barriers. It jumps hurdles, leaps fences, penetrates walls to arrive at its destination full of hope."[1] Those words captured perfectly my experience with pure love— the kind that builds us up, binds us to one another, and helps us recognize our own inherent worth.

For years following my paralysis, I struggled to love my own reflection, wondering if I would ever find someone who could do the same, wheelchair and all. When Jay came into my life, he showed me that love is all-encompassing, that it perseveres through all circumstances. Just as I relied on my family's love to support me through my initial injury, I now found myself made stronger because I had a loving partner by my side as I moved into a new chapter of life once again. While I fought my way through the darkness of my surgeries, love for my sport motivated me to keep going. While I fought my way back through the darkness of my emotions, love from my husband and my family did the same thing. Despite all my struggles and doubts, Jay's love for me never wavered, and what was more, he was waiting for me on the other side when I finally figured out how to love myself again.

That love gave me a safe place to come back to when fears and sadness overwhelmed me; that love let me catch my breath, rest my soul, and gather up my courage to return to the fight. No matter how unworthy or how unlovable we may feel, we all deserve to experience the depths of love. Love is the only thing I know of that can reach us at our absolute bottom and help guide us back toward the light. Love in its many forms—love of another person, love of a pursuit or a passion, love of yourself—is the force that not only obliterates every limit but proves that these limits truly don't exist.

ELEVEN

EMBRACE YOUR COMEBACK

"I can't," I frantically told Jay.

"Yes, you can, Mal. Just breathe," he calmly responded.

I tried with all my might to catch my breath, but I felt myself drowning in my own anxieties. *Breathe*, I thought to myself. *Breathe.*

There I was, in PyeongChang, South Korea, and I felt consumed by the isolation of my hotel room. It wasn't set up like a typical hotel; it was more like an apartment building with an empty lobby that led to a hallway lined with individual rooms. The Paralympic opening ceremonies were still a few days away and most of the media had not yet arrived. Not only did the building feel empty, but it was also at the top of a hill, away from the village where all the other buildings and restaurants were located. In the half hour since my NBC colleagues had assisted me to my room, the only living thing I saw pass by my window was a cat. A single cat.

Now, with each gasp for air, I felt my heart race as I choked through my own tears. My mind was outpacing me even though I was fighting to slow it down long enough to regain control. I'd been afraid of isolation before, but I'd never actually *been alone* for longer than a few hours since my arm surgeries, and now it was as if every emotional scar from the past four years was fighting to make itself known.

Jay was also in PyeongChang, managing a production crew for a documentary we were developing, but since I was working as a correspondent for NBC, we weren't staying in the same hotel. As my anxiety attack seized my body and mind, I forced myself to reach for the phone to call Jay. I could hardly speak when he answered, and he knew immediately what was happening and encouraged me to start taking deep breaths to calm myself.

"I can't. I can't do this," I heard myself repeating, and within those words lay the very fear I had been trying to silence since my arm injury. What if this time was different, and rather than thriving the way I did following my paralysis, my injury got the final word?

A few minutes later, my heart rate and breathing slowed. Jay had to go. "I love you, Mal. You're going to be okay. I promise," he said as he hung up. Cradling my phone, I curled up in a fetal position on the couch, rocking back and forth, trying to anchor myself in my surroundings to stay grounded and in the present. A few minutes later, Jay called back: "NBC is going to relocate you to one of the buildings in the main village where everyone else is staying. It's all right. You're okay." His calmness was reassuring; yet, as I came back around to reason, I felt defeated—like I should be able to control my emotions better than that. The fear turned to anger and shame for having such a big reaction to an emotional trigger I'd believed was behind me.

I wanted so badly to move beyond what happened to my arm on March 5, 2014; yet here I was, four years later, still struggling with the emotional scars from that day. A few hours later, as I got settled in my new room down in the village, I felt a tiny glimmer of clarity. There it was, the answer I'd been looking for: "Control the controllable." I began organizing my belongings—something to hold me in the moment and, more than that, something I could control. I looked out my windows and saw the light reflecting off the snow. All I could see was dazzling, blinding white all the way up the mountain. It wasn't quite the same as the serenity of a black line, but it represented the vastness of possibility that lay before me and the promise of peace on the other side of my fears and anxieties.

Just about six weeks earlier, NBC had offered me a commentator position for the 2018 Paralympic Games, making me the first American woman in a wheelchair to serve in such a role. The significance of reporting from my wheelchair wasn't lost on me, because that simple act was about something so much larger than myself. Following my paralysis, I yearned to see representation in the media of people who looked the way I now did, living full and fulfilling lives. It's difficult to become what you don't see. Outside of my career as a Paralympic athlete, I felt like every way I turned, there was a void—a missing link between diversity, inclusion, and the disability community. Deep down, I knew my role represented something much more signficant than simply reporting: it would help shine a light for a community that, in America, is drastically underrepresented.

My job in PyeongChang was to conduct interviews at the base of the mountain in what is called "the mixed zone," which is just a fancy way of saying the media corral where athletes pass through immediately following competition. I was assigned to alpine skiing and snowboarding, and while I had learned how to monoski years ago, both my assigned events were pretty foreign to me. Rather than allowing the unknown to spark insecurity and anxiety, however, I relished the idea that for the six weeks before I left, I had the opportunity to learn about the sports while I prepared for my first major role as an on-camera reporter.

"These aren't the same as the interviews I have conducted in the past. Those were behind camera, in documentary format, not on camera for broadcast," I expressed to Jay, just a few days after accepting the gig. There was no preparing myself mentally for how to conduct a nationally televised interview.

"You'll be amazing, babe," Jay assured me, supportive as always.

I spent the next month compiling research on all the athletes competing in the sports. I quizzed myself relentlessly on their hometowns, past wins, and rivalries. I pored over every article and online bio I could find, trying to commit every fact to memory. I even spent most of the fifteen-hour flight to South Korea rereading all the stats and stories that filled the binder I'd created. When I arrived in PyeongChang and met my crew from NBC, I was excited to show them my prep work. Mo, my amazing producer, looked from me to my binder and back to me; finally, she gave me a wry smile, laughed a little, and asked, "Um, you do know that we have a whole team of researchers who do that work for you, right?"

I did not. But at least now I felt extra *extra* prepared for my upcoming interviews. As for my binder, I still carried it with me each day. I didn't just want to get it right; as an athlete myself, I knew the amount of sacrifice, heart, and soul the athletes had put in just to get there. If I was going to be on the other side of the camera, sharing in some of their greatest moments of success or deepest moments of heartbreak, I had a duty to do their stories justice.

Despite all my preparation, though, I was left terribly shaken by my anxiety attack when I first arrived. I wanted to snap back into reality and tell myself I was more than my fears, but, of course, self-shaming doesn't help. All I could do was ground myself to reality and do my best to keep moving forward. "Control the controllable," I reminded myself every day as I settled into my routine and prepared for day one of competition.

Minutes before my first broadcast, my crew and I arranged ourselves in our little eight-by-eight-foot corral at the bottom of the slopes. Mo handed me the microphone and said, "Here you go. Let's do this."

Let's do this, I repeated in my head. *I can do this*. *I can do this*.

I saw the red light flash on the camera, got my cue, and began to speak. By the end of my introductory segment, I couldn't erase the stupid grin on my face. Throughout the day, as I talked with each athlete following their runs down the mountain, my face ached from smiling, but I couldn't stop. I felt more at ease with myself than I had in years. Sometime toward the end of the afternoon, I glanced over to see Jay watching me. He and his crew were at the mountain filming, and he stopped to observe me working for a moment. There was something so powerful about knowing that on the side of that mountain we were chasing our dreams together. "Seeing you completely in your element, so happy and self-assured, I was so proud I wanted to cry," he told me later that night. "This is everything I ever wanted for you."

Leaving PyeongChang, I felt as if I had crossed some invisible boundary of confidence. Despite my panic on the first day, I found the strength to control what I could and not let that moment define my entire experience in South Korea. I had tapped into the power within myself to do what needed to be done in that moment. Sometimes, those seemingly tiny victories are the very things that change our direction, shift our focus, and realign our perspective. Instead of obsessing over the light at the end of the tunnel, we can look for the light that fills it—that little glimmer that tells us there is strength, beauty, or hope right here, right now, in the midst of the darkness. The darkness is not all there is. There is always *something* we can do to survive the moment, just as there is always something on the other side of our fear to which we can cling.

———

About a month later, when Jay and I traveled to London for business, we made sure to carve out time to visit the London Aquatics Centre—our first time back since the 2012 Paralympic Games. As we entered the facility, I could feel every emotion rush back: the heartbreak of my reclassification, the joy of becoming a Paralympic champion. That pool deck held pieces of my heart. After changing into my suit, I sat behind the block of lane two, the very lane in which I won my gold medal, and reflected on everything it represented to me. Then I took a deep breath and dropped into the water. As I hovered above the black line, I realized how much had changed over the past six years, including my own body. It was as if I could close my eyes and relive those final meters of my race all over again. My hand met the wall, and I could feel the emotions that engulfed me on September 2, 2012, but the only person in the stands this time was Jay. He was the first one I called after my race then, and that friendship had turned into the deepest love I have ever known. London will always hold a piece of my heart, and it serves as my reminder that love and faith are the forces that drive us through even the greatest of odds and lead us to the other side, where good really does overcome.

I carried that thought with me into the water after we returned home and started swimming again that spring. It was slow going at first, but I held on to the confidence that I had the power to push through the worst of times to create something beautiful.

That summer, the Minnesota Vikings moved into their new practice facility, which is adjacent to a state-of-the-art training center called Training Haus and located in my hometown just outside Minneapolis. Each time we drove by, Jay would say: "Mal, we should go check it out one day!" I always responded with a vague, noncommittal nod. I was still so far away from where I wanted to be that the idea of a new training facility just seemed like too much to consider. But he kept nudging me gently in the direction I was meant to go, even if I didn't know it yet. Next thing

I knew, we were setting up a meeting to tour the facility. That was all it took, and Training Haus became my new "home away from home." Though my strength and conditioning workouts weren't what I was used to, Russ, my physical therapist, got more and more creative with each session, finding the fine line between pushing my body within its parameters while also meeting my body where it was. That balance fueled me and gave me strength—not just physically but mentally—and matched the size of my ambition. I wasn't simply looking to once again qualify for the national team; I had my eyes squarely locked on chasing Paralympic gold. Ever since I sat atop the podium in 2012, I had dreamed of doing it again, even if I had to build my career from the ground up for a third time.

The challenge, of course, was that I hadn't just lost muscle mass in my eighteen months out of the water; I'd straight-up lost muscles—as in, they weren't in my body anymore. My surgeries the previous year had removed or detached a number of muscles in my neck, chest, and upper arm. I was starting from scratch and creating a whole new chapter in my career—relearning training techniques, adapting to my new body, and rebuilding the essential swimming muscles that had become severely deconditioned since I left the pool in fall 2016.

I learned a lot about humility as I fought my way back to competition shape once again. The reality is, you can't be arrogant if you want to stage a successful comeback; you have to be willing to start from zero. You can't let your ego or your past accomplishments tell you that you don't have to pay your dues. There is no halo effect or favoritism when it comes to training; your past successes don't allow you to skip steps along the way. Your body doesn't care how many records you've broken or medals you've won before; in order to get back into the game, you have to start exactly where you are with what you have—even if that means starting over completely. There's simply no bypassing the system.

I'm not going to lie—it wasn't easy to swallow my pride. I had never been bothered by racing against little kids when I first started swimming following my paralysis, because I knew I had to begin somewhere. But now, every time I swam, it was a reminder of how far I was from where I used to be. It felt as if I had reached the summit of a mountain, and instead of *just* getting knocked back down to the bottom, the entire path that I carved out on the way up was taken out as well. I knew this time around I would have to forge a new way forward full of twists, turns, switchbacks, and detours— but I also knew, deep down, that I had the power to become more than I had ever been. This comeback wasn't about returning to where I once was; it was driven by a desire to accomplish more than ever before.

Each day brought new strides as well as slides backward. But I learned that there is a difference between steps back and setbacks; sometimes, in order to move forward, we have to take a step backward and readjust before we can proceed. In our sessions, Russ and I slowly started introducing strength and conditioning movements in addition to our physical therapy exercises.

In the pool, Steve eased into allowing me to ramp up both my intensity and distance. The deal was that as long as my body could handle it, we would proceed. "Smarter, not harder," he insisted. As difficult as it was to be patient with my slow progress, my passion for the sport proved stronger than my desire to get back on top of the podium once again. I was motivated by the fight to get there, not by the allure of the podium itself. I rooted my drive in everything that swimming gave me: freedom, confidence, and the courage to keep going. That, I believe, is where grit comes into play; it's the essential fuel of any comeback.

Grit is showing up to the fight when you don't have any fight left in you. It's falling seven times but getting up eight. Grit is the characteristic that makes people say, *"Really?"* when they see you get knocked down face-first and still find the inner strength to come back for more. When people talk about comebacks, they usually use words like *drive, dedication,* and *perseverance.* The truth is, drive will carry you *to* a comeback, but only grit will push you *through* it. There is simply no substitute for grit—not wishing, not good intentions, not vision boards or positive thinking, not even hard work. Those things are great, of course, but if they aren't coupled with tenacity and a willingness to pick yourself up off the ground, time and time again, they can't take you the distance. And that's exactly where I was going in fall 2018, when I tightened my goggles and put on my cap to race for the first time in two years.

At a small developmental meet outside Los Angeles in September 2018, I got on the blocks again for the first time since Rio, and I did . . . okay. I certainly wasn't turning heads, but I was hitting my goal times. Steve and I knew I couldn't expect to just jump from where I was to where I wanted to be overnight, so we created incremental steps—goal times that gave me a target and allowed me to feel a sense of accomplishment. I had a long road ahead of me, and I needed to create opportunities for little wins along the way to prevent me from going down the rabbit hole of "comparison with past Mal." It is so easy to get lost in comparing ourselves to where we once were or what someone else is doing, using it as a metric to justify telling ourselves we aren't enough. The only problem is, when we do that, *nothing* will ever be enough. A comeback is rooted not just in challenging your body but also in changing your perspective.

Was making a comeback physically challenging—even excruciating at times? Absolutely. But the mental recovery was even harder because I had to break free from the comparison mindset. Those micro-goals helped me stay focused on the way forward. With my husband and parents cheering in the stands, I raced in that small meet: my first goal. Was it a win? Nope. Was it a victory? Absolutely. So I kept going. The next stop was nationals in December.

But those months weren't only about training. In a sudden and completely unexpected turn of events, Jay and I stumbled upon our dream home in early October, after months of looking for an accessible house to call home and coming up empty-handed. You quickly realize how important turn radius, doorway width, spacing between counters, and floor transitions are when you are moving about on four wheels. We finally decided we would need to build a custom home and began the long process of selecting a lot and narrowing in on design elements. Then, out of the blue one weekend, Jay noticed a new listing and asked if I wanted to take a look. I didn't. I was too emotionally exhausted from constant training for nationals and constant disappointment with the home-buying process—falling in love with a house online only to discover that my wheelchair didn't fit through the doorway or that the kitchen would need a complete overhaul just for me to be able to reach the counters. Reluctantly, I looked at the pictures and agreed that it looked promising; so we called our real estate agent and made an appointment for the next day.

He met us on the front porch grinning, and said, "I think this is the one." As I entered through the front door, I instantly imagined our future there. The floor plan was open and easy to navigate. The flooring flowed seamlessly from one room to the next, which made rolling easy. The kitchen was perfect in every sense: low storage, enough space between the counter and the island so Jay and I could cook together, and the counters were exactly the right height for me to reach without Jay having to stoop over. But the best part was that I didn't have to think twice about my wheelchair as we toured the home; I just moved about freely. The main living space was all on one floor. We went back out to the front porch, where a bright red swing hung, and Jay and I sat together for a moment. I looked out to the yard and envisioned our future kids playing with our Lab, Sam, on a Saturday morning. I glanced over to the front door and could feel the warmth that would flood our porch as we welcomed loved ones. This wasn't just a house; it transformed into a home before my eyes.

This was it. We'd found the perfect place to build our family and raise our kids. It was five minutes from my parents, equidistant between my training pool and Training Haus (ten minutes in opposite directions), and less than twenty minutes from the airport, which was great given how much we travel.

Jay and I had to fly to Los Angeles three days later, so we

prayed about the decision, crunched our numbers, and submitted an offer just hours before we left for the airport. We knew it was wishful thinking, but we decided to leave our text messages on for the flight just in case our agent received any information while we were in the air. Somewhere over Colorado, my phone buzzed. Our offer was accepted and the closing could be fast-tracked. We would move in on October 31—three weeks away.

With a tiny bottle of airline champagne, we toasted to ourselves as homeowners and to that little God-wink of a home more perfect than what we could have planned ourselves. In the coming days, the enormity of our decision sank in, and I began asking myself all the questions: What would I do when Jay had to travel without me? Were we ready to live without the assistance of my parents? *Did we just make a huge mistake?* But then I remembered that, for the first time in years, I would be able to take a shower without having to drag myself up a set of stairs. If I forgot my phone on a different floor, I wouldn't have to ask someone else to get it for me. I wouldn't end up stopping halfway upstairs, crying, because I wished I could move through my own house with ease. I would even be able to carry a cup of tea around with me wherever I wanted to go—something I couldn't do in a house with steps. As limitless as my public life seemed, my private life would finally reflect that as well. And with that, I realized this wasn't just a house; it was the answer to years of prayers.

Jay and I hosted Thanksgiving that year, and my family kept teasing me that I didn't have to do everything, even though in true "I do it" fashion, I did. "You cooked," they insisted. "We can do the dishes." What they didn't understand was how much of a joy it was simply to be able to reach the sink myself or go and grab another bottle of wine from the fridge. For years, I'd had to rely on other people not just to do the hosting but to care for me in times when I couldn't tend to myself. Yet here I was, listening to the laughter echo through our home and feeling pride as I watched my husband carve the turkey we had cooked in our own kitchen. The young, scared girl first learning how to navigate a wheelchair had built a career, but even more than that, she had created a home, made it her own, and welcomed others in. Sitting around the table with the people I loved most in the world, reflecting on the things for which we were the most thankful, I felt as if I had everything I could ever want: love, home, and the chance to launch my career again. This was so much better than any simple comeback. I wasn't back where I left off, but I was in a new and infinitely better place.

A few weeks later, I flew to Tucson for nationals alongside Jay, my parents, and Steve. On December 17, 2018, I won the 50-meter freestyle—my first national title since 2012. It wasn't a career personal best, but it was faster than in September. And this time it wasn't just a personal victory; it was a full-blown win! With each race my confidence grew, and I felt tiny slivers of myself return. I was still navigating through the depths of the emotional toll of my injury, but each little success along the way allowed me to feel glimmers of the light that surrounded me. Immediately, I focused on the next goal: Indianapolis in April for the World Para Swimming World Series (it's a mouthful!), which also would serve as our qualifying event for world championships the following fall in, of all places, London. The goals I had set as metrics had only grown alongside me, and the next two on my list were making the national team and climbing the world rankings high enough to make our world championship team. Lofty? Sure. But I left nationals thinking, *Why not me?*

In March 2019, Andrew Parsons, the former chairperson of the Paralympic Committee of Brazil, was elected the new president of the International Paralympic Committee (IPC), and one of his priorities was making improvements to the classification system. That meant all para-swimmers worldwide would have to be reevaluated using new and more standardized guidelines. This would be my first opportunity for review since the London 2012 Games. My appointment was set for April in Indianapolis. Since my last reclassification from an S7 to an S8, quite a bit had changed with my body, and while that was difficult to come to terms with, I anticipated it would affect my overall evaluation.

The week leading up to that meet brought so many mixed emotions. My grandfather passed away on March 24, and our family gathered together to mourn. Two days later I turned thirty, an age where many athletes start talking about retirement rather than gearing up for a third act. Four days after that, on April 1, I was sitting on a pool deck in Indianapolis, waiting for the review committee to finish their evaluation of my medical records and physical exam so they could make a decision about my classification. I held my breath as the classifiers walked over and informed me of the official ruling: S7. I was back in my original class, where I hadn't raced in nearly seven years. I struggled to hold back the tears, which came from the relief that my body's trauma was recognized and validated, the grief that I still wasn't completely at peace with my new body, the fresh sense of loss at my grandpa's death, the uncertainty of what this new classification meant for my career, and the excitement of what still lay ahead of me. Those tears carried a lot of different emotions as they rolled down my face. I still had no idea whether I could maintain a steady climb back to the top of my class, but I knew everything that had happened over the previous years had been a part of getting me to that point, and I was going to race with everything I had.

Five days later, as I took the starting blocks for the 50-meter butterfly, I couldn't help but reflect on the fact that it was almost eleven years to the day that I reentered the water for the first time following my paralysis. When I touched the wall 35.72 seconds later with the fastest time in the world for that race, I knew that this comeback had been worth every frustrating moment as I swallowed my pride and fought my way back from the bottom. And this was only the beginning.

Seeing my name on the board with a 1 next to it and realizing that I was ranked first in the world, despite every setback along the way—knowing that I could have given up a million times and no one would have blamed me—was the sweetest feeling I could imagine . . . but being back on the national team was awfully close.

———

In June I traveled to Los Angeles for the Angel City Games, an event designed to introduce families to the world of adaptive athletics and teach individuals with various physical abilities the power of sport. It was my second year as a volunteer, coaching clinics and mentoring incoming athletes. There is something so powerful in the way sport can transcend the field of play and change lives, and that weekend served as a reminder that we all have the fundamental right to play, regardless of our perceived abilities.

The 2019 Angel City Games were especially significant for me, because I had the chance to race the 50-yard butterfly and ended up breaking the American record—one that had been standing since 2010, held by yours truly. It wasn't just that I broke my first record in seven years or that I broke a record of my own *that had stood for nine years*; I had beaten my old record with a body that had been through the ringer—proof the limits never truly existed in the first place. This comeback was taking me to new heights beyond any I had reached before. And the icing on the cake? Jay was there to witness it—my first record since we had become a couple. We have a photo from that day, just moments after I pulled myself out of the pool. My legs are still in the water as I sit on the edge, my face is scrunched up into a huge smile, Jay is reaching over to give me a high five, and a wheel from my chair fills the bottom left quadrant of the foreground while the desert sun bleaches out some of the color. It perfectly captures the genuine joy of the moment, and it reminds me that dreams can survive even the darkest seasons.

That summer the board of directors of the US Olympic Committee (USOC) unanimously voted to change their name to reflect the inclusion of all Team USA athletes, becoming the US Olympic & Paralympic Committee (USOPC). Ever since its inception, more than half a century ago, the US Paralympics had operated under the umbrella of the USOC; now we received full recognition as part of our shared sporting body. What was more, they became the first committee in the world to include both the Olympic and Paralympic names in their title.

"The decision to change the organization's name represents a continuation of our long-standing commitment to create an inclusive environment for Team USA athletes," Sarah Hirshland, the CEO of the USOPC, announced. "Paralympic athletes are integral to the makeup of Team USA, and our mission to inspire current and future generations of Americans. The new name represents a renewed commitment to that mission and the ideals that we seek to advance, both here at home and throughout the worldwide Olympic and Paralympic movements."[2]

IPC president Andrew Parsons agreed, celebrating the move as "a historic moment for the Paralympic movement in the United States. To see the USOPC make this inclusive statement by changing its name demonstrates the true parallel nature of the Olympic and Paralympic movements."[3]

The Paralympic movement was finally getting its due, and I couldn't wait to be a part of the next chapter. This kind of inclusion was beyond anything the nineteen-year-old girl watching the 2008 Paralympic swim trials could have imagined, and everything the thirty-year-old woman she grew into now dreamed of.

In my training, though, I was doing much more than dreaming. Five days a week, I woke up at 5:00 a.m. to be in the pool at 6:00 a.m. for two hours of swimming with Steve. Then it was a quick shower and off to Training Haus for another hour and a half of conditioning and body work with Russ. By the time I got home a little before noon, I was beyond beat. Sometimes I curled up in a fetal position on my closet floor, too exhausted to put on "real clothes." Sam sometimes nosed his way in and curled up next to me, as tightly as a yellow Lab can, in what I can only assume was a gesture of solidarity. I was now at the point of training so hard that my body literally shut down following workouts, but I heard Russ's famous words on repeat in my head: "You've got this, Mal! You can do anything for ten seconds." Through each training session, either in water or on land, I would play those words on repeat: *Ten seconds. You've got this.*

Anyone who thinks the life of a professional athlete is all glitz and glamour has clearly never caught a glimpse behind the scenes of competitive training. But I knew what all this pain, exhaustion, and effort was for. I understood now that swimming was a gift; there was no guarantee it would stay in my life, no promise that it would be there for me tomorrow. After being forced to stay out of the water and out of racing, I was determined never to take swimming for granted again. For so long, *all* I could do was visualize the pool; now I knew I should count it a privilege that I was in the pool before sunrise each morning, even though I'm definitely not a morning person. Each day represented a new opportunity to become better, to chase a long-awaited dream for which I had fought so hard; therefore, I got up and trained—not always with a smile, but always with every ounce of effort I could muster.

On September 2, my plane touched down at Heathrow Airport for the 2019 World Para Swimming Championships. Here I was, back in London, seven years to the day since I'd won Paralympic gold, and at the same pool where I was just a week away from racing again. And *that* was the last major international meet before the Tokyo Paralympic Games in 2020. It felt as if my journey from the top of the world to the depths of despair was finally coming full circle, and I, for one, couldn't wait for competition to begin.

After taking the bus across the country to Wales, Team USA settled into our dormitories at the Swansea University to begin our station camp, where we take a few days to adjust to the time change, get over jet lag, and practice ahead of competition. My first night there I felt the beginnings of a panic attack coming on, but instead of spiraling, I reached out for help and was able to breathe my way through it. The effects of anxiety are definitely not my favorite things in life, but I have come to accept that they just might be a part of who I am now—my emotional scars are every bit as real as my physical ones. That doesn't mean they control me, and they certainly don't define me. They simply are a reminder that I've been through some rough times and I've made it through to the other side. I taped photos of my family and notes from my tribe on my dorm wall, and I reminded myself that I was never truly alone.

On our final afternoon in Swansea, I had some free time to explore and found myself sitting in a quaint café, watching light struggle tirelessly to pierce the overcast sky. It seemed like a fitting metaphor. I thought about my journey, my comeback, and the fact that this meet and all the promises it held were an extremely long time coming. As I tend to do in those moments of reflection, I pulled out my journal and started to write.

It has been nine years since I have represented Team USA at a world championships, seven years since I have sat atop a major international podium, three years since I have raced internationally, and over two years since I have felt like myself. Now I sit in this café knowing that despite it all, despite everything I have faced I am here. I have overcome. . . . I feel ready in a way I never have before. I can envision the next ten days and they don't scare me. I feel in control—calm, collected, and confident—this feeling of knowing that magic is about to happen and nothing feels forced. So, for now, I sit and watch the clouds as the sun breaks through, as if I am being reassured from above that this is my moment—the moment I have been prepared for.

A few days later, as I rolled onto the pool deck of the London Aquatics Centre for the start of the competition, I thought back to my two previous experiences here—the emotional roller coaster of the 2012 Games and my visit the year before when my career was still a big question mark. *This is what I fought for,* I thought, breathing in the clean smell of chlorine and admiring the beauty of the venue all decked out for competition.

My first event was the 50-meter butterfly, and after placing first in prelims that morning, I waited eagerly for finals. Sitting in the ready room, though, I didn't feel myself getting psyched out. Instead, I felt a pervading, all-encompassing sense of calmness. I wasn't nervous, I wasn't scared, and I wasn't worried. It wasn't that I thought I had the race in the bag—I knew I had a target on my back and that every single one of the other seven women brought her A-game to that race. No, the peace I felt was rooted in something bigger than the race; I felt powerful and in charge of my body, my mind, and my destiny. Instead of my old pre-race song, "All I Do Is Win," this time, I played a remix of "Survivor" by Destiny's Child as I rolled onto the pool deck when my name was called.

Approaching the blocks, I couldn't help but think about what my teammate Joe Wise had said to me the last time I raced in this same pool: "Go shock the world." This time, I was swimming only to shock myself. The fact that I was back in the water at all was a miracle, let alone ranked the number one seed going into finals at the world championships. I faced my fears, I moved forward, and I redefined my own limitations time and time again. I failed. I overcame. I believed myself worthy of fighting for. And all that time, I had been surrounded by an amazing community of support and love. The horn sounded; I hit the water with the full force of my journey pushing me ahead and the magnetic draw of a limitless future pulling me forward. Each stroke was a victory. Every time I rose from the water, it was as if I was rising above all of the pain that held me down for so long. My lungs filled with air and my mind emptied itself of doubt. No matter what happened in this race or in my career, nothing could take away everything I had given to come back to this moment—*my* moment.

As I touched the wall and rose to the surface, I glanced at the board: "M. Weggemann: 1." It took at least a full second before I grasped what I was reading. Even the replay of the event shows the moment or two of my incomprehension before it hit me. I was a world champion once again, for the first time since 2012, despite everything that had happened and all I had struggled to overcome. Looking at the stands, I saw my mother giving the thumbs-up she always sealed with a kiss, my dad waving an American flag and jumping up and down, stoic Steve shaking his head and grinning, and Jay—my rock, my pillar, my partner—going crazy. I felt the last of the darkness that had lingered for so long finally melt away. These were the people who had never let go of me or of my dream; in fact, they held on to it all the tighter when I was at my lowest. I had come back—not just to racing, not just to the top of the podium—but, as I looked at the sheer joy on the faces of the people I love, I knew I had the power to come back to the light too.

Just as we have a choice in how we will react to our circumstances, we also have a choice in which way we will allow the water to take us when it closes over our heads. Will we sink or will we rise? Over the next five days at Worlds, I won another gold and a silver. But it wasn't the medals that marked my true comeback; it was the sense of fullness, acceptance, and peace with myself that I'd been struggling to find for so long. That's the beauty of comebacks; they aren't just about the tangible metrics but who you become along the way. Each fork in the road leads you in a new direction, allowing your comeback to take you to places you've never been before. Now, at last, I saw my way forward clearly enough to finally reach the other side.

———

No one ever tells you, "Swim toward the light." People just take for granted that your body will want to rise to the top, that it will instinctively fight the natural pull of gravity taking you down, sinking you until you settle on the bottom. The air bubbles know; they are a model of efficiency, shooting straight upward until they reach the surface and disappear. The light shows us which way is up—the way to break through the surface and return to the sweet, sweet air that gives us life.

I had found it once, so I knew I could find it again; but for too long, I'd been far below the surface and desperate for air. I ached to reach the light above me, but I didn't know how. I knew that it was love that lifted me, carried me, and gave me direction—and now, I could feel my body rise upward toward it. My legs that felt nothing, my arm that felt too much—they rose with me because my body knew intuitively that this was what it was supposed to do. I had to surface to live; there was no other option.

I was determined to come back, so I locked my eyes on the lights, on the love that surrounded me, and I rose.

TWELVE

WRITE YOUR OWN ENDING

For me, it was a black line that bridged my past to present and led me towards my future—it showed up in the form of the line which trails the bottom of the pool and the one which trails these pages within my journal. Over the years, I have used these two passions, swimming and writing, to create a path forward—to give that day meaning and purpose.

—FROM PERSONAL JOURNAL, JANUARY 21, 2020

Returning home from world championships in fall 2019, I felt as if a weight had lifted, and for the first time in years I could see clearly. Adding my fourteenth and fifteenth world championship titles to my résumé meant more than winning a few races. For years I yearned to return to where I had once been, but while navigating through the darkest season of my life, I also found my truest self. Through the process I was reminded that dreams are resilient and have the power to withstand even the greatest storms; you just have to choose to keep showing up ready to fight. That's what I did, day in and day out, for years on end—even when I couldn't seem to surface, even when I couldn't find the light. I had survived because I found the courage to believe that something inside me was superior to circumstance.

In September 2019, coming off Worlds and less than a year from the start of the 2020 Paralympics in Tokyo, I couldn't help but reflect on how different I felt from four years prior. Going into the Rio 2016 Games, I didn't know whether or not I would even be named to Team USA. This time, I was a gold-medal favorite with a bull's-eye squarely on my back. For some, that pressure can feel all-consuming, but I drew strength from challenging myself not only to stay on top but to defy expectations, pushing myself to be better than even I thought possible. That was my goal for the Tokyo Games—to fearlessly chase down my dreams and see just how far I could rise.

There are two ways to view the future: *What if?* and *Why not?* Looking forward through a lens of *What if?* subconsciously places limits on our potential, anticipating failure rather than allowing ourselves to see the vastness of possibilities that lie before us. On the other hand, *Why not?* recognizes we have an inherent right to chase that dream, no matter the odds, and it roots our goals in a mindset where anything is possible.

The choice is ours; but for me, I decided to keep looking ahead by asking myself the latter. Why *couldn't* I become a Paralympic gold medalist again? Why *shouldn't* I chase down my own world record in the 50-meter butterfly that had stood since 2012? Who's to say I can't be better than I have ever been, despite an injury that means I should be weaker? Sure, I have had muscles removed from my arm. No, my nerves don't work the way they should, and that limits my strength in certain muscles. Here's the thing: adaptability is a powerful tool, and I *know* how to adapt. Mental strength can carry you further than physical strength alone. And when you have nothing to prove, you also have nothing to lose. Who cares if I fail? Not me. Through all I have traversed, I've found an inner strength—strength that doesn't depend on a gold medal or a world record. Falling short of my dreams doesn't equal failure, because I now know that the only true failure is not allowing myself to dream in the first place. Whatever power my body may have lost, my mind seemed to have found; so I was going to push my way forward, guided by that inner strength. Of course I'd love to reach the top of the podium again, but not because I want the accolades; I want to prove that I have what it takes to fight for it.

As I entered the fall of 2019, laser-focused on the 2020 Paralympic Games, I did so stronger than ever before. The year-long buildup to the Games is always an exciting time, marked by celebrations as athletes finally get a chance to show the world the fruits of our dedication and sacrifice during the years when no one was watching. For a short period the world joins in—as if they are cheering us on in the final push to the finish line.

Early in October 2019, just three weeks after I got back from London, I was invited by the USOPC to help make the official announcement that the Paralympic super trials (swimming, track and field, and cycling) would take place in the Twin Cities the following June, with the University of Minnesota aquatics center hosting swimming. That announcement was exciting for a lot of reasons, but it carried special significance for me. Not only had I just launched back onto the world stage at the very pool where I first claimed Paralympic gold in London, but now I would be competing for a spot on Team USA at the same pool where I first watched trials as a newly paralyzed teenager in 2008. Following the press conference, I went to the University of Minnesota aquatics center with local reporters and spoke about the significance of that pool. I pointed to the lane where I took a leap of faith and swam for the first time just two and a half months after my paralysis. Then I looked up to the wall behind the stands, to the Minnesota Swimming Hall of Fame, where my own plaque hung in the very spot where I used to sit during my sisters' meets when I was a little girl. It was as if I could see my entire journey play out on that pool deck, and now I would have the chance to be named to my third Paralympic team in the place where it all began. Everything seemed so perfect—scripted, almost. I had no idea of the challenges that lay ahead.

On the heels of the super trials announcement, I was invited to NBC's West Hollywood (WeHo) pre-Olympic and Paralympic photo shoot and press junket. There, a few of Team USA's Olympic and Paralympic contenders spent several days doing photo shoots, interviews, and filming promos on roughly twenty different soundstages. Representatives from Getty, *People* magazine, and other major media outlets attended the event as NBC prepared to roll out its full Olympic and Paralympic hype machine. The energy at WeHo was unbelievable, and whatever excitement I already had about Tokyo was amplified tenfold.

As Thanksgiving came and went, I continued my training for

Tokyo, which meant more than just physical training. I wanted to use my growing platform as a force for good, doing my part to change perception of disability in our society and paving a path forward for future generations, just as powerful athletes before me had. Beyond medals, I strive to leave a legacy that allows the next generation not only to see a path forward but to never have to ask, "What about me?" I want to do my part to create a world for our children that doesn't define "normal" by one single metric, to fashion a society where children won't be told their mommy is "different" just because she lives with a disability. My purpose is to use what was the darkest day of my life for good.

The first week of December, I had the honor to return to the United Nations for International Day of Persons with Disabilities to speak in the main chamber. My message centered on increasing visibility and inclusion for our world's largest underrepresented demographic: the disability community. My desire, I explained, was for every individual to have the power to determine their own destiny in a world free of societal barriers. I believe it is not only within our power, but it is our duty to create a world that *all* can access—regardless of race, religion, perceived ability, gender, or sexual orientation. My call to action was not limited only to creating accessibility, but also to fostering true inclusion that allows everyone's voice to be heard equally.

Less than two weeks after the event at the UN, I moderated a panel at the premiere of a documentary produced by TFA Group, the social impact agency and production studio that Jay and I cofounded in January of 2019 and for which we serve as co-CEOs. Our mission is to use the power of storytelling as a catalyst to change the world by inspiring and empowering our audiences to take action in their own lives. As an athlete training for a Paralympic Games, a motivational speaker, an advocate, a co-CEO of a company, and an executive producer on various production projects, my plate was incredibly full—but it was full of passion and purpose.

If all that wasn't enough excitement leading into one of the biggest years of my career, I also realized it was finally time to tell my story in a new way. Through my speaking career, I found that vulnerability ultimately connects us. My story of navigating through the depths of loss while allowing hope and resilience to carry me forward resonated with people exactly where they were. So I decided, on top of everything else, it was time for me to write a book.

Remember my trip to the Mall of America with my dad back in 2008, just a few weeks after my paralysis, to buy a new pair of shoes for physical therapy? The trip where I realized I didn't see a single person whose body looked like mine? One afternoon in December 2019, I had just rolled into the shoe department of that very same Nordstrom when my literary agent called to tell me that the book had sold. I sat for a long time after that call, tears running down my face as I reflected on how much had changed in the past eleven and a half years. Instead of soft, flat moccasins to ease myself into learning how to put shoes on, I was trying on a pair of fierce, block-heeled booties for a professional event; I had traded my hospital room for the boardroom. The girl who had sat in this same place nearly twelve years ago had been terrified of her future and yearned to see hope somewhere, in someone else; now she was living a future richer than she could have dreamed, and filling that void herself.

The whirlwind of the last few months left me breathless in all the best ways. It didn't seem possible that a life that had felt so blank and hopeless at nineteen could now be so full. Society had told me to expect loneliness, frustration, and emptiness going forward, but my life had only grown in excitement, opportunity, and love. Never had I understood more deeply the importance of writing my own ending rather than accepting the narrative of what my story was "supposed" to look like.

As the calendar turned to 2020, I put my head down and fixed my eyes on two things: Tokyo and my book. Steve, Russ, and I began ramping up my training and nutrition to maximize my body's output for the next eight months, and I could feel myself growing stronger and faster each day. Athletes often talk about "putting on the blinders" to focus entirely on the upcoming competition, and that was exactly what I did. I heard snippets of news stories on the radio each morning as I drove to practice or while I cooked dinner in the evenings, but nothing really captured my attention because my mind was fixated entirely on trials, Tokyo, and writing. If anything major was going on in the world, it didn't fully register; I was so hyperfocused on my goals that the outside world just felt distant.

Even my work outside the pool was tied to the Games. In January, I proudly wheeled myself down the red carpet at the Golden Globes as a guest of Gold Meets Golden, a group that merges Olympians and Paralympians with Hollywood superstars to highlight achievement in both industries. On March 2,

2020, I flew to Los Angeles to join Michael Phelps, Kerri Walsh Jennings, Allyson Felix, and Ibtihaj Muhammad as Delta Air Lines announced its role as the inaugural founding partner of the LA 2028 Games, taking over as the official airline of Team USA in 2021. The shift in sponsorship was huge, and I was thrilled to be a part of such an important moment that signified the continuation of the Olympic and Paralympic spirit into the future.

I had two more trips scheduled for speeches over the next week and a half, and when I traveled I noticed a distinct shift in the way people were interacting with one another. I've always carried disinfecting wipes in my bag for cleaning my seat on an airplane (in a Games year, no one has time to get sick, so we all tend to go a little overboard), but it suddenly seemed like nearly everyone was doing the same thing. No one was shaking hands; instead, elbow bumps became the greeting of choice. Everyone flinched when someone coughed in a public place. The night before I left to fly to Florida for our national team camp, the NBA announced that two players had tested positive for COVID-19 and suspended the rest of the season. In the back of my mind, I knew what that likely meant for the rest of the sports world, but I couldn't allow myself to take off those blinders.

⸻

"Who do we swim for?" shouted one of my teammates.

"U-S-A!" the rest of us echoed in return.

On March 14, day three of camp, we lined up two athletes per lane at the wall to begin our test set. We were to swim full-out for 100 meters, then sit at the wall for a few minutes as the lactic acid built in our bodies, checking our heart rates periodically; a quick recovery in heart rate signifies strong aerobic capacity. We repeated this seven times, pumping one another up as we waited for our next round.

"Come on, Mal! How bad do you want it?" Hannah, my teammate, called.

"You got this! Come on, Hannah, why not you?" I shouted back as we both pushed off the wall to start our next set.

"Mallory, 1:11.72," one of our coaches hollered as I touched the wall.

"Say that again?" I asked as I caught my breath.

"1:11.72," she repeated. In my shock, I almost forgot to check my heart rate. While I had managed to make strides in certain events, my 100-meter freestyle had remained at a standstill for the past four years. But now, in the middle of a test set with my teammates, my body beaten down from travel and having pushed off the wall rather than diving off the block, I clocked my fastest 100-meter freestyle time since before the Rio 2016 Games.

Again, I thought to myself. Sure enough, on the next round I went even faster: 1:11.49. I couldn't stop grinning. With Tokyo right around the corner, my body suddenly found a way to improve on my biggest competitive challenge. This was it. This was my year. I could feel it in my bones. My teammates and I continued to cheer one another on. As a team, we finished our test set and felt our bodies give us a glimpse of the performances that lay ahead of us that summer across the Pacific.

When we all got out of the pool that evening, our coaches

called us together for an unscheduled meeting before we departed to go back to the hotel. Despite our Games blinders, there was no tuning out the global conversations happening over the past few months, so most of us knew what was coming. But we held our breath anyway, praying we were wrong. "Due to the recent events with COVID-19, the USOPC has decided to suspend all travel," Erin Popovich, associate director of the national team, told us. "Your tickets that were booked for next week will be rebooked for tomorrow instead. You will all return home." Her voice cracked a little; the magnitude of the decision was not lost on anyone. We all looked at one another, the same sinking feeling apparent on everyone's face, and the same question at the forefront of everyone's mind: *What would this mean for Tokyo?*

When I got back to Minnesota that Sunday, my sisters, Jay, and I gathered at my parents' house for one last hug before the lockdown orders went into effect in the coming days. The next twenty-four hours felt like a blur. I went to my training session with Russ, but rather than getting in the strength session we had planned, we spent that morning doing as much soft-tissue work on my arm as possible to get it in the best shape we could for the next couple of . . . weeks? months? . . . until facilities began to reopen. Closures had not yet begun, but we knew from our friends on both coasts that they were coming. *Prepare for the worst and hope for the best*, I told myself as we talked through our potential plans.

There was still no official announcement regarding a postponement or cancellation of the Games, so we had to make decisions as if things were going forward as scheduled. Swimming with Steve later that afternoon, I pushed myself as hard as I could, and my body responded. I could feel my speed in the water, and I knew I had crossed some invisible barrier in my training.

"Mal, you need to slow down or I'm taking you out of the pool," Steve chimed in, trying to rein me in a bit. "You're going to trash your body, and you'll be useless the rest of the week."

Desperate to make the most of what could be my last time in the pool for who knew how long, I challenged him. "That's assuming we have a pool the rest of the week."

Steve wasn't amused. He gave me a time that, instead of being a goal time to try to beat, was actually a "slow down" time that would require me to pull back. "Do not go faster than this, or I'm leaving and you can bury your body however you want on your own," he snapped.

I knew he was serious, and I understood his reasons, but I also hated the feeling of having to force my body to slow down just as I was reaching new heights. I still refused to believe that the Games would be affected. The pending shutdowns would be temporary, and everything around Tokyo would go forward as planned. I was sure of it.

The thing is, my stubborn denial wasn't just about my athletic comeback, though that was obviously a major factor. Jay and I wanted to begin to try for a family following Tokyo. We knew it wouldn't be simple; in fact, a few years ago we found out that in order to have children, we will have to embark on our own fertility journey. Following my paralysis, one of my greatest fears was that I wouldn't be able to have children. Once I found out I could, I felt incredible relief. Honestly, it was the one question I was most afraid to ask. Society assumed that if I have a spinal cord injury, then I automatically must not be able to conceive or give birth. Both are completely untrue, yet somewhere along the way, I began to believe they might be.

I still remember sitting in the doctor's office when Jay and I finally got up the courage to ask my physician about my ability to have children—and the complete and utter joy we felt when we learned how deeply wrong those assumptions were. However, with time we found that fertility struggles can arise for many reasons, and while my paralysis wasn't a factor, it didn't mean there wouldn't be obstacles. We were concerned that Jay might have some fertility challenges, so we decided to go through testing, and we grieved what felt like a very real loss as we reviewed the results together. But we also understood that families are created in many beautiful ways. We learned that infertility is something that affects roughly one in eight couples and can come from the man, the woman, or both sides. It isn't something to hide or be ashamed of; it doesn't make us less-than or inadequate—it simply is, just like any other physical condition.

It took time, but after coming to terms with our new reality as best we could, we knew my body would be in the healthiest condition of my life immediately following Tokyo, so it seemed like the right time to begin the IVF process. This would give us time to relish the first few precious baby years before I had to transition back to training mode for 2024, since my athletic dreams don't end until I see my husband and our children cheering me on in my final race at the LA 2028 Games.

That evening, Jay and I went over to Steve's house to have dinner with him, Shelly, and the girls. While we were there, the governor announced that Minnesota was immediately shutting all bars, restaurants, and fitness facilities while moving toward a shelter-in-place order in the coming days. We watched the press conference together in grim silence, then I excused myself from the room and wheeled into the entryway of their house while everyone else started on dessert. I didn't want anyone to see me cry, especially not the girls. But I felt a tremendous amount of grief in that moment. I still clung desperately to the hope that this would all blow over by the end of the spring and that the Games would still go forward, but I also understood that I couldn't set my heart on that. Even if the Games *weren't* postponed or canceled, how could I continue training without a pool and still hope to be competition ready in August? How much longer could I hold off painting our nursery before the emptiness overwhelmed me?

After one of the darkest seasons of my life, I had finally returned to the light, and I didn't want to sink into darkness once more. Yet I couldn't help wondering: How many more times would the rug be pulled out from under me? How many more curveballs could my heart stand? Suddenly, I felt Shelly wrap her arms around me in a big hug. I looked up and saw Jay and Steve behind her. "We've got this," Steve said in a stern but reassuring voice as he put his hand on my shoulder. We made our way back into the kitchen and joined the girls. All it took was a reminder of the support that surrounded me, and I realized I had all I needed. My doubts vanished just as quickly as they had surfaced.

Before Jay and I left that night, we came up with a plan—one that required flexibility, creativity, and lots of trust. The next day, after a couple of phone calls, Jay and I drove all over town loading up our van with equipment. We picked up a VASA trainer (also known as a "swim bench," which allows you to replicate strokes without being in water) that was lent to us by a member of the community. Training Haus let me borrow kettle bells, medicine balls, and resistance bands—all items that Russ had built into our new training program. The gym Steve co-owns pitched in with a rower and a few more weights. We quickly set up a gym in our garage, and Steve began coming over every day for socially distanced training. While I worked on my strokes, he sat in a lawn chair six feet away and coached me on my technique. After a few days, however, we transitioned to distance training, and I forged on alone.

We settled into our new routine, and by week two I found myself sitting beneath the VASA trainer with a roll of black tape in hand, carefully replicating the black line on the bottom of a pool on my garage floor. Hovering over the black line has long been my sanctuary. It is where I retreated to grieve my paralysis, where I found life following loss; it is the place where I have navigated the depths of heartbreak, where I found the courage to forgive, where I fearlessly chased my dreams, where I feel like my truest self. For swimmers, the black line serves as a point of reference for both where you are and where you are going. The line doesn't extend all the way to the wall, but rather it stops in a T, 1.6 meters away— an indicator either for a turn or a finish. The line can't carry me all the way to the wall; it can only point the way. Ultimately, the ending is up to me. Re-creating that black line on the garage floor was a reminder that while I "swim" in place, it doesn't mean I stop fighting for every inch. Regardless of whether or not the wall is within reach, I need to continue to show up each day, following the line through every stroke as it guides me forward.

Just a week later, I was getting ready to shower after my morning workout when I heard my phone buzz. Glancing down, I saw a breaking news banner: "Tokyo 2020 Games Postponed to 2021." I sat for a moment or two in my bathrobe, staring at the screen and trying to process it. As long as the postponement had been just rumors, I could cling to the hope that everything would still be okay. No longer. My athlete blinders could shut out reality for only so long. I knew there were far more pressing matters in the world, and I knew things could be worse in a million different ways. But, in that moment, my heart hurt deeply, and my sadness was real and valid.

I sat in the shower with my elbows on my knees and my head in my hands as the water rushed over me. I looked at my body and all it had been through, and I asked myself, *To what end? At what point do the sacrifices amount to more than the end goal you are sacrificing for?*

Afterward, wrapped in my robe, I wheeled into my closet to get dressed and passed the alcove in our room where I'd been dreaming of placing a bassinet. I broke down a second time; this time because my heart so deeply felt the loss of knowing I would not be launching on the road to motherhood in six months. The postponement meant my lifelong dream of becoming a mom would have to wait another whole year. This was one of the toughest blows. This pandemic wasn't just threatening one life-defining goal of mine; it seemed to be hitting me on multiple fronts.

My sobs were so loud that sweet, loyal Sam came to my side,

licking my face and offering comfort. Before I knew it, Jay had come in too. There all three of us sat—Jay embracing me with Sam at our feet—as we felt every ounce of grief for the life we thought would be, for the magnitude of the sacrifices we had made for my career. We did everything we could to prepare for what we had envisioned, but in the end, the timing wasn't up to us. That is the thing about learning to rewrite your ending—life is unpredictable. You can be headed down one path, then, in a split second, it can all change with a quick glance at our phones, with an unexpected call, with a single devastating phrase, in the blink of an eye in a procedure room, with a fall in a shower. These sudden moments of impact can change everything in an instant.

This is true for all of us. I knew that this season of heartache would pass, and that the pain I felt that day was building my strength for the next morning, when I would pull myself up, wipe my eyes, and keep pushing ahead. I also knew that this was not the last time I would have to face a sudden heart-wrenching change in direction. None of us can control what is going on in the world; all we can do is decide how to bring light to our corner of it.

A few hours later, the USOPC sent out an official email confirming the postponement. With that last sliver of hope extinguished, I lifted my head and shifted my focus. I chose to use the gift of an extra year of training as time to grow stronger both physically and mentally. I also found ways to push myself professionally, starting a weekly series on Instagram Live called "Spark a Conversation." I began interviewing prominent figures in the sports and disability community on an array of topics from mental well-being to adaptability and resiliency to the power of media as a mechanism for change. I resolved to become more outspoken in advocating for representation for the disability community. And I accepted that if I could not look forward to beginning the journey to motherhood for at least another eighteen months, I would find another way to birth a part of myself into the world. You, reader, are holding the result of that labor in your hands.

Yes, I was already writing this book before the pandemic began, but as I sat down to finish it in the spring of 2020, I realized how much my journey paralleled what countless people were feeling in that very moment. The world suddenly found itself in a brand-new, frightening, and unknown situation—something I understood all too well. As the spring wore on and summer approached—the summer that should have marked the culmination of years of heartbreak and tears with joy—I poured myself into every page and every word you've just read. I adjusted my training schedule to accommodate my writing. And, as I pondered my new trajectory and what I could take away from this unexpected time, I, very literally, rewrote my ending.

I had been incredibly excited for trials to take place at the University of Minnesota, at the same pool where I first discovered my love for swimming as a child, where I first saw elite athletes who looked like me as a young adult, where I first felt freedom in the water again. That is where this book was supposed to end, with me being named to my third Paralympic Games at the very place it all began. But that's not the way my story is going to go right now; *no one's* story is going the way they planned right now.

We are all rewriting our stories at this moment. As I put these words on the page, the United States is just now stepping out of a spring filled with feelings of isolation, fear, uncertainty, anger, and righteous protests following the senseless death of George Floyd. While it feels as if we are all starting to come back out into the world after being in social isolation, the effects of this season in our lives will carry forward for years to come. Over the past several months, people have lost jobs and companies they've worked a lifetime to build. People have lost their homes due to financial devastation. People have lost a feeling of connectedness while they struggled to maintain a safe distance from their support structures. They've lost a feeling of security in their own communities. And, of course, so many, many people have lost their lives or those they love in the face of what is occurring in our world right now.

Every one of us is surrounded by *so much loss*, every day. We all face sudden moments of impact—those unforeseen, unexpected, life-altering moments that send our lives on a trajectory we would never have dreamed of. Our legacy, however, is not defined by those moments but by the choices that come after. We write our own stories through the decisions we make every single day to rise above, adapt to, or redefine whatever knocked us off one course and onto another.

Throughout this time of uncertainty, I have heard countless individuals ask the same question: "What if life never returns to what it was before?" It is a valid question, and one that we all will find ourselves asking following a sudden moment of impact as naturally we yearn for everything to return to "normal." But the reality is, we may never return to what life once was, although that doesn't have to mean we can't become more than we have ever been before.

When I was first paralyzed, I prayed with all my being that my life would return to what it was on January 20, 2008—the day before my life changed. I thought the only way forward was by going back to a time when everything seemed to make more sense. I came to learn, though, that looking ahead was actually the only way forward. Yes, I am still paralyzed. Yes, I have faced my fair share of additional hardship and loss since. But as I write this, it is a beautiful summer evening in June, and I am sitting on my deck with my dog, Sam, at my side while my husband stands at the grill, making us dinner. I am content; even more than that, I am satisfied, happy, fulfilled, and surrounded by so very much love. In this moment, I know that the only way forward is through.

Somewhere along the way, I learned that hope isn't about holding on to a fantasy that everything will "fix" itself; hope doesn't guarantee that our greatest dreams, wishes, and desires will come true—but it does guide us forward. Hope allows us to know, deep down, that regardless of what our circumstances bring, we have the strength to carry on.

We all must face the depths of heartbreak, navigate through loss and uncertainty, regardless of how painful it might be in the moment. This is a necessity for becoming who we are meant to be. Your world may never return to what it was prior to your sudden moment of impact, and your life might be forever changed—but maybe, just maybe, it is this very hardship that will carry you forward beyond anything that you dared dream possible.

I don't know where the path takes me from this moment forward, but I do know that my heart is filled with hope and rooted in faith. It is in times like these when the power of resilience comes into play for all of us. Our job is not to understand exactly where the journey will take us—we just have to show up, day after day. It isn't about wishing for life to return to what it was; it is about embracing what it will become.

We are all facing a sudden moment of impact right now, and we have the opportunity, both collectively and as individuals, to decide what we are going to do with it. Not responding is not an option. The ultimate question is *how* we will respond. How will we use this, or any other unforeseen challenges in our lives, to propel ourselves forward? To be the best we can be? To make a difference? To change the world?

Here's a secret: you don't have to have an answer to any of those questions right now. And here's another secret: those answers might change at any time. But the one thing that never, ever changes is the fact that you have a say. You have the choice. You have the power. You get to write your own ending.

And *that* is what makes you limitless.

ACKNOWLEDGMENTS

When I was first paralyzed, I yearned for clarity, wanting to understand the *why* behind January 21, 2008. What I came to understand is, that day uniquely positioned me to find a deeper purpose than I ever imagined—but that journey wouldn't have been possible without the love and support of many people. It is because of each and every one of them that I am beyond grateful for that day in 2008; in many ways, it brought more love into my life than I even dared dream possible. Not only would I not be who I am without those remarkable individuals, but *Limitless* wouldn't have been possible without them. Each one has guided me, taught me, challenged me, and anchored me—they have given purpose to my life.

Words will never do justice to the gratitude I hold for the entire team at Nelson Books and HarperCollins Christian Publishing. Thank you to Webster Younce for taking a chance on *Limitless*, for empowering me, and believing in my story—you paved the way for one of my wildest dreams and allowed me the honor of answering my *why* within the pages of this book. Thank you to

ACKNOWLEDGMENTS

Jenny Baumgartner for carrying this story forward and your end-
less passion. And to the entire team: Sara Broun, Kristen Golden,
Shea Nolan, Kristina Juodenas, Sujin Hong, and everyone else who
has left their fingerprints on *Limitless* throughout this process—
thank you, I couldn't ask for a better team of individuals to bring
these pages to life.

Bringing this story to life wasn't just about fulfilling my dream
of becoming an author, but sharing my story in a way that I hope
can empower others to find their own limitless potential within—
and that would have never been possible without one incredible
woman, Cassie Hanjian. Thank you, Cassie, for being my champion throughout this process. You were not only my literary agent
that brought this dream to life, but you became a teacher and a dear
friend. *Limitless* is beyond lucky to have had you as its advocate.
And to Reiko Davis, thank you for seeing this journey through and
guiding me along the way. I am beyond grateful for both of you
and the entire team at DeFiore and Company.

I have always believed you are only as good as the people you
surround yourself with, and I have seen those words play out as
truth, time and time again. Tiffany Yecke Brooks, you are one
of a kind, and I am beyond grateful for your wisdom, guidance,
friendship, and strength. We have dreamed of writing this story
for years, and in that time, you have become so much more than a
cowriter; you are a dear friend. I am a better person because of you,
and *Limitless* is a better book because of you. Thank you for all
you are—you have been my strength throughout this process, and
there was no greater honor than to go through it with you. And
to Bridget, you, my dear, deserve all the gratitude in the world for

being our biggest cheerleader and leading with curiosity. It is my hope that you know how deeply you have influenced this book for the better, serving as a reminder of what we want our next generation to become, believing in the promise of tomorrow, knowing that we are worthy of all things splendid in this world, and seeing a path forward.

To think back on the past twelve years since my paralysis and to know the depths of love that has surrounded me in that time, I am forever grateful. When I found my way back to the water following my paralysis, I was guided by not just a coach but a mentor. Thank you Jim Andersen (Jimbo) for empowering me to find my own limitless potential within. You not only led me to the top of the Paralympic podium, but you helped me find my way back to life following my paralysis.

It takes an incredibly special person to meet you where you are and believe in you regardless of a specific outcome. For me, that individual is my coach, Steve Van Dyne. It is because of you, Steve, that I found my passion for the sport of swimming in the first place—years ago as a teenager on the Eagan High School pool deck. To think back and realize how far we have come, and what we have accomplished since, is a testament to your unwavering support. Thank you Shelly, Ashley, Paige, and Alexa for believing in this dream and seeing it through with me. I know, no matter which way the tides turn, I have your support, and for that I am grateful.

To each and every member of my community who has filled my life with color, who showed up from day one and wrapped me with love—I am who I am because of all of you. To Katie, my best friend, you have been there through it all, and I am beyond grateful for your friendship. To Roxane, for being there on April 8, 2008, and lending me a suit as I returned to the water for the first time; it was through that simple act that I was able to find the courage to follow through on what became the biggest pivoting moment in my journey. To the coffee ladies, thank you for being my mom's dearest friends and always showing up for our family. To our church community who built a ramp, filled our kitchen with meals, and surrounded us in prayer. To the swimming community who welcomed me back with open arms and helped me find my path forward. To my fellow Team USA teammates for constantly empowering me, reminding me of the power of sport to transcend the field of play and reach our communities. To my sponsors throughout the years who have continually supported my dreams. You have all enriched my life and given my purpose meaning, reminding me of my *why*, and for that, thank you.

As the years have passed, I have been blessed with a family that has grown. Thank you to my mother and father-in-law for raising the man I am fortunate enough to call my husband and for supporting me as your own since the beginning. I am beyond grateful to have your love and support throughout this journey. To my sister-in-law, thank you for your selflessness and willingness to travel far and wide to show up for those you love. And to my brother-in-law and family, thank you for all you have done. I am beyond grateful that with Jay came the addition of such a supportive and loving family.

I have always dreamed of how I would thank my parents, what I would write, the words I would use, and none of them seems to adequately express the gratitude I hold in my heart for all they are and all they have afforded me. Mom, you have been my anchor, reminding me at every turn that *good overcomes*; meeting me with a thumbs-up, regardless of what the day has brought; and always willing to greet me with chicken, rice, and cheese hot dish and a hug when I need them most. And Dad, your wisdom has guided me through the most unbearable times and grounded me through the most triumphant. Thank you for instilling in me the belief that we all have the power to make a difference and change the world. Thank you to both of you for all you have done, all you have seen me through, and having the courage to let go twice and empower me to find my way forward.

My sisters, Christin and Jessica, we have been through so much, but we have always navigated through them together. I truly do not know what I would do without the two of you. Thank you for being my role models; I have looked up to both of you since day one, and I always will.

And last, but certainly not least, my love, every day I am grateful that our worlds collided. I never knew if I believed in serendipity, but then you came along, and it was as if a greater power kept bringing us together. Being your wife is one my greatest honors; I love you with all that I am. Thank you, Jay, for believing in me and my wildest dreams, for your unwavering love, and for being the type of man that makes everyone around you better—to know you is to love you. You have been my light through some of the darkest of days—every low is softened and every high is heightened with you. I love the little family we have built with our fur-baby Sam and the dreams we hold for our future children. Which leads me to Sam, our loyal, loving Labrador, who has seen me through the last decade and been by my side through every step of this process, giving me snuggles and kisses at every turn. You fill our life with so much joy, and I am beyond grateful for our little family of three.

Life is about filling our days with love, knowing that all moments are bigger than ourselves, and that our greatest purpose in this world is to be true to who we are. To each and every one of you, thank you for opening your heart to my story. It is my greatest hope that, throughout, you were able to honor your own.

NOTES

1. Maya Angelou, "Love recognizes no barriers. It jumps hurdles, leaps fences, penetrates walls to arrive at its destination full of hope." Facebook, January 11, 2013, https://www.facebook.com/MayaAngelou /posts/10151418853254796.
2. Sam Carp, "USOC Rebrands as US Olympic & Paralympic Committee," SportsPro, June 21, 2019, https://www.sportspromedia.com/news/usoc -rebrand-us-olympic-paralympic-committee.
3. Carp, "USOC Rebrands as US Olympic & Paralympic Committee."

ABOUT THE AUTHOR

MALLORY WEGGEMANN is a world-record-setting two-time Paralympic swimmer for Team USA. She has set fifteen world records and thirty-four American records. She is also the recipient of an ESPY Award, a fifteen-time world champion, and a Paralympic gold and bronze medalist. Weggemann served as a commentator on NBC for the PyeongChang 2018 Paralympic Games. She has established herself as a leader outside the pool as well; she is an inclusion advocate serving on the Advisory Board on Disability for Delta Air Lines as well as a cofounder and co-CEO of TFA Group, a social impact agency and production studio. A highly sought-after motivational speaker for Washington Speakers Bureau, Weggemann has presented at numerous Fortune 500 companies, including Bank of America, Morgan Stanley, Comcast, PepsiCo, Northwestern Mutual, Aetna, Deloitte, and Delta Air Lines. She resides in Minnesota with her husband, Jay, and their beloved dog, Sam.

TIFFANY YECKE BROOKS has worked as a lead or contributing writer for nearly two dozen books, including *Fear Is a Choice* with

ABOUT THE AUTHOR

Pittsburgh Steelers running back James Conner. She holds a PhD in literature from Florida State University and teaches writing courses for several universities. She lives in Oklahoma with her family.